THE MORTGAGE ON THE ELGIN MARBLES

O. M. Lewis

Published by High Tile Books Ltd, 2016

www.hightilebooks.com

A CIP catalogue record for this book is available from the British Library

ISBN: 978-0-9954953-3-3 (print)

ISBN: 978-0-9954953-2-6 (ebook)

Cover design by Averill Buchanan

Text design and typesetting by Averill Buchanan

Printed and bound in Great Britain by Clays Ltd, St Ives PLC

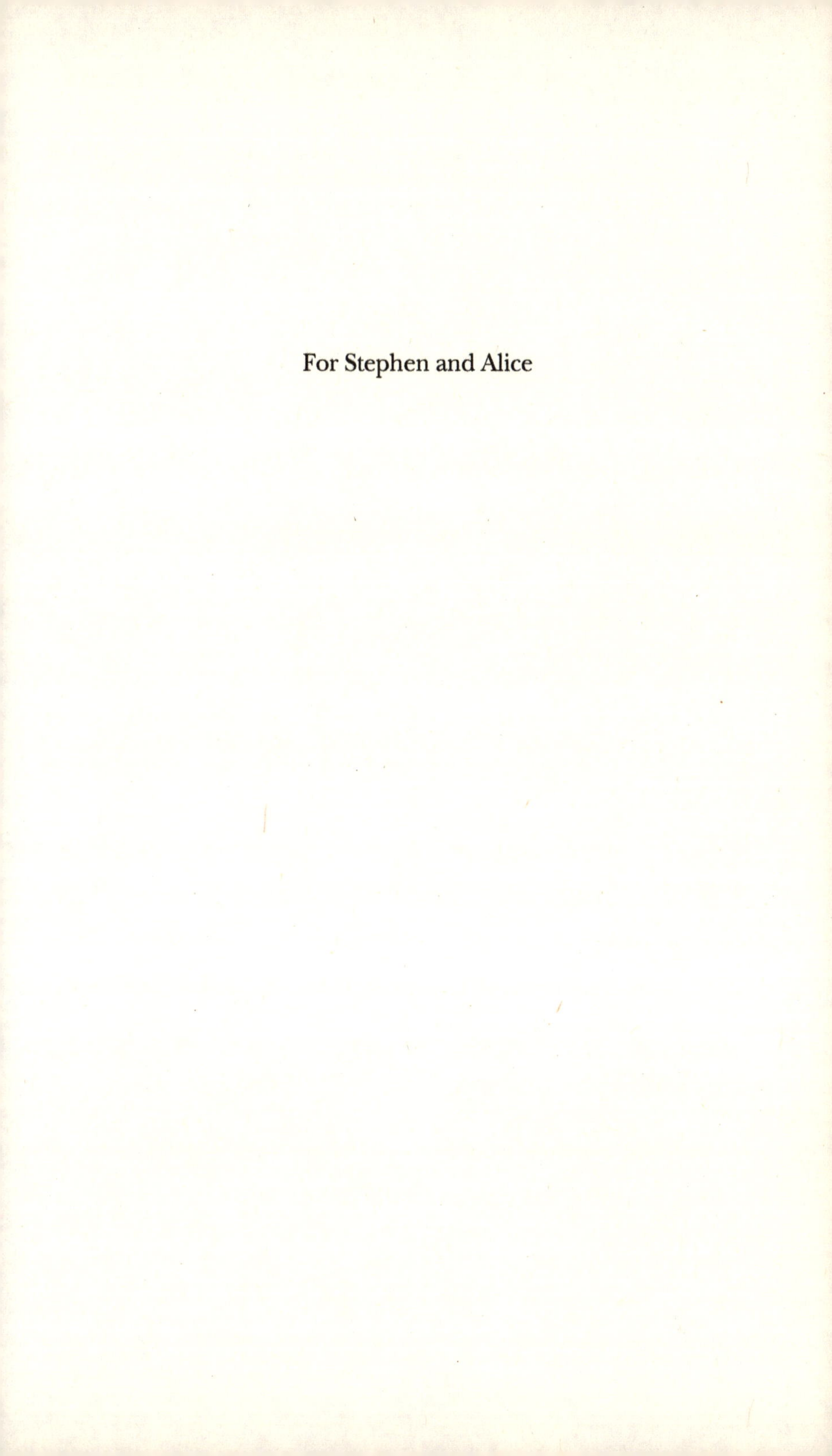

For Stephen and Alice

CONTENTS

Acknowledgements

I would like to thank:

Lucy Aliband for her drive, comments on countless drafts and constant support.

Daria Prigioni for her comments and advice on the manuscript.

Averill Buchanan for editing, proofreading, typesetting and indexing the book, and designing the cover.

Rebecca Souster at the printers, Clays Limited.

My son and daughter, Stephen and Alice, and many friends for their encouragement and support during the writing of this book.

Abbreviations

ADM:	Admiralty
C:	Chancery
FO:	Foreign Office
NA:	National Archives, Kew, London
T:	Treasury
TS:	Treasury Solicitor

CHAPTER 1

Sculptures of marble from the Parthenon

Ancient Greece is considered to be the greatest civilisation the world has ever seen, and the Parthenon in Athens is thought to be the supreme monument of Greek antiquity. The Parthenon was built around 447 BC as a pagan temple; it then became a Christian church in the 5th century AD, and from the early 1460s, after the Ottoman invasion of Greece, it was used as a mosque.[1]

In 1799, Lord Elgin was appointed British ambassador to the Ottoman Empire (now Turkey).[2] At the time, Greece and Athens were under Turkish control. Elgin removed sculptures from the Parthenon, and between 1801 and 1812 they were transported to England by ship. The sculptures are known as the Elgin Marbles or the Parthenon Sculptures.

Some people claim that Elgin did a good deed, that he saved the sculptures by taking them to England; if he had not done that they would have been destroyed. However, this is clearly mistaken because if Elgin had left them where they were, on the Parthenon, they would be in the Acropolis Museum in Athens today with the sculptures he did not take.

For over two hundred years historians, academics, writers and journalists (and more recently politicians and lawyers) have been consumed by the overriding and all important matter of whether Elgin had the necessary permission to take the sculptures. The British Museum maintains that its case for

---

[1] The change of use was not unusual. For example, the Hagia Sophia in Istanbul was built in AD 537 as a Greek Orthodox basilica, converted to a Roman Catholic cathedral between 1204 and 1261, and was a mosque between 1453 and 1931. In 1935, it was secularised and today is a museum.

[2] Lord Elgin: Thomas Bruce (1766–1841), 7th Earl of Elgin and 11th Earl of Kincardine. He was ambassador to the Ottoman Empire from 1799 to 1803.

retaining the Elgin Marbles cannot be challenged because Elgin had permission to take them. The Museum further maintains that arguments to support the removal of the marbles are based, in part, on discrediting Elgin and his actions.[3]

This book is not concerned about permission, nor does it attempt to discredit Elgin or his actions. This book explains how the Elgin Marbles were acquired by the British Museum in 1816, irrespective of whether Elgin had permission to take them or not.

How the British Museum acquired the Elgin Marbles is pertinent to the debate about whether it should retain them or return them to Greece as requested by the Greek government. However, it is not an aspect of the debate that has been extensively covered to date. Only two explanations have been previously published. The first is by A. H. Smith, who published his long essay 'Lord Elgin and his Collection' in 1916, the centenary of the acquisition by the British Museum.[4] Smith was in a unique position to write about the acquisition of the Elgin Marbles. He was not only related to the Elgin family, but he was also Keeper of Greek and Roman Antiquities in the British Museum. He had access to both the British Museum's and Elgin's papers, the latter made available to him by the Earl of Elgin, Elgin's grandson.[5] The second explanation is by the historian William St Clair, whose book *Lord Elgin and the Marbles* (1967) relies heavily on Smith's account.[6] In this book, reliance is placed on Smith where he and St Clair cover the same ground.

When Elgin sold the marbles to the British Museum in 1816, the trustees of the museum did not pay the sale price to Elgin. This is because at the time of the sale the marbles were held by

---

[3] 'The Parthenon Sculptures: Facts and Figures.' *The British Museum.* 2008. <www.britishmuseum.org/about_us/news_and_press/statements/parthenon_sculptures/facts_and_figures.aspx>. Clause 10. Last accessed: 17 October 2014.

[4] A. H. Smith, 'Lord Elgin and his Collection', *Journal of Hellenic Studies*, 36 (November 1916), pp. 163–372.

[5] Smith, 'Lord Elgin and his Collection', p. 163.

[6] In the first edition of his book, published in 1967, St Clair acknowledges that he relied heavily on Smith's work, and says that where he gives no authority for his own statements they usually derived from Smith (William St Clair, *Lord Elgin and the Marbles* (Oxford: Oxford University Press, 1967), p. 275).

the British government as security against money it had advanced to Elgin between 1800–1802 while he was British ambassador in Turkey. The contention in this book is that Elgin used the money he received from the government to remove the marbles and that the government knew what Elgin was doing.

The government did not seek to recover the money it had advanced to Elgin until 1815, when it became apparent that parliament might not grant the British Museum the funds needed to buy the Elgin Marbles. So the money advanced to Elgin by the government thirteen years previously was used as a device to create a mortgage over the Elgin Marbles (dated 4 December 1815; see Chapter 16), and the government seized the marbles as a precautionary measure.

The existence of the mortgage over the Elgin Marbles has gone under the radar for two hundred years. Smith devotes forty-two pages of his essay to 'Purchase Negotiations' between the British Museum and Elgin, yet nowhere does he mention that there was a mortgage over the marbles when they were acquired by the British Museum. The British Museum's own document, 'The Parthenon Sculptures: Facts and Figures' (2008), in which it corrects what it describes as 'Further common misconceptions', also omits any mention of the mortgage.[7] However, some of the British Museum's facts, figures and corrections are factually inaccurate to the point that the museum's case to retain the Elgin Marbles discredits a great institution.

How and why the mortgage came to be created has a significant bearing on the way in which the British Museum acquired the Elgin Marbles and on the two hundred-year debate.

---

[7] 'The Parthenon Sculptures: Facts and Figures.' *The British Museum.* 2008. <www.britishmuseum.org/about_us/news_and_press/statements/parthenon_sculptures/facts_and_figures.aspx>. Last accessed: 25 July 2016.

CHAPTER 2

The Parthenon Sculptures or the Elgin Marbles?

Before explaining how the marbles got into the British Museum Elgin deserves a leg-up, because he takes a number of falls. With regard to Elgin's legacy, the marbles in the British Museum should properly be known as the Elgin Marbles and not as the Parthenon Sculptures. This is because an Act of Parliament in 1816 stipulated that when the British Museum obtained them they should be called 'The Elgin Marbles'.[1]

Another of the 'Further common misconceptions' is that the British Museum calls them the Elgin Marbles. It does not. It says its preferred term is the Parthenon Sculptures. Chiselled into the wall of the Duveen Gallery, which houses the sculptured marbles from the Parthenon at the museum, are the words, in large letters, 'The Sculptures of the Parthenon'.

The British Committee for the Reunification of the Parthenon Sculptures (one of twenty-two national members of The International Association for the Reunification of the Parthenon Sculptures) states on its website that it considered it a victory when the British Museum stopped referring to the marbles as the Elgin Marbles and started calling them the Parthenon Sculptures. However, the Parthenon Sculptures is a misnomer for the Elgin Collection of Marbles acquired by the British Museum in 1816.

The Parthenon is one of a group of buildings on the Acropolis of Athens. Other buildings on the site include the Temple of Athena Nike, the Propylaea, the Erechtheion and the Theatre of Bacchus. Elgin took marbles from all these buildings on the Acropolis and they are in the British Museum.

---

[1] *An Act to vest the Elgin Collection of ancient Marbles and Sculpture in the Trustees of the British Museum for the Use of the Public* (1816). 56 Geo. 3, c. 99, pp. 865–867.

The Elgin Collection of Marbles acquired by the British Museum in 1816 consists of:

- eighty-two marbles from the Parthenon;
- four from the Temple of Athena Nike;
- seven from the Propylaea;
- eighteen from the Erechtheion (including the Caryatid Marbles and the iconic column from the Erechtheion);
- four from the Theatre of Bacchus;
- thirteen detached heads;
- thirty-four detached pieces of sculpture (one from Constantinople);
- eight altars;
- thirteen sepulchral pillars;
- sixty-six Greek inscriptions;
- a lyre and two flutes made of cedar wood found during the excavations among the tombs in the neighbourhood of Athens;
- hundreds of urns discovered in digging ancient tombs round Athens; and
- a collection of 880 Greek coins (66 gold coins, 577 silver and 237 copper).

The objects in the Elgin Collection of Marbles acquired by the British Museum are listed and described in the *Report from the Select Committee on the Earl of Elgin's Collection of Sculptured Marbles; &c.*[2] The report, referred to here as the Select Committee Report, lists sixty-six Greek inscriptions in the Elgin Collection of Marbles, but there were considerably more. C. T. Newton, Keeper of the Greek and Roman Antiquities at the British Museum, wrote: 'By the purchase of the Earl of Elgin's Collection of Marbles in 1816 upwards of a hundred highly interesting inscriptions, mostly from Athens, were acquired by the Museum. This collection included the celebrated Sigean Inscription, one of the most ancient examples of Greek palaeography in existence.'[3]

---

[2] *Report from the Select Committee of the House of Commons on the Earl of Elgin's Collection of Sculptured Marbles; &c.* (London: W. Bulmer, 1816), pp. 70–7.

[3] C. T. Newton, ed. *The Collection of Ancient Greek Inscriptions in the British Museum* (Oxford: The Clarendon Press, 1874), n.p.

The Greek inscriptions acquired by the British Museum from Elgin were sawed from blocks of marble using stone-cutting saws, leaving behind mutilated buildings. Five of the inscriptions were sawed from the Parthenon and four from the Erechtheion.[4]

Sydney Checkland, who had unfettered access to the Elgin archives at Broomhall, the family's ancestral home in Scotland, wrote that Elgin sent a dozen marble saws of different sizes for use on the Parthenon. The central East frieze, for example, required twenty-foot saws to cut it up.[5]

Some of the pieces taken from the Temple of Athena Nike, the Propylaea and the Erechtheion are on display at the British Museum (Room 19); the remainder are in storage. All of the marbles in the British Museum collection that were taken from the Parthenon are said to be on permanent display.[6] However, Elgin was not the British Museum's only source of marbles from the Parthenon. Fragments of the Parthenon came to the museum from another ten sources (see Chapter 23), and it is unclear whether all are on permanent display. Furthermore, the inscriptions taken from the Parthenon by Elgin are not on display.

The gold coins in the Elgin Collection include a rare 'Daric and a didrachm of Philip Arideaus with the type of Alexander the Great'.[7]

Today, the trustees of the British Museum would prefer, unsurprisingly, that Elgin's name was not associated with the sculptured marbles taken from the Parthenon. The Greek government and people would prefer, unsurprisingly, that the marbles taken from the Parthenon were returned to Athens.

The marbles taken by Elgin will here be called the Elgin Marbles, which shall refer not only to the sculptures taken from the Parthenon but also to the entire Elgin Collection of Marbles

---

[4] The text and translation of each of the inscriptions is in Newton, ed. *The Collection of Ancient Greek Inscriptions in the British Museum*, Part 1, from p. 35; also in Adolf Michaelis, *Der Parthenon* (Leipzig: Druck und Verlag, 1870–1), pp. 295–9.

[5] Sydney Checkland, *The Elgins, 1788–1917: A Tale of Aristocrats, Proconsuls and their Wives* (Aberdeen: Aberdeen University Press, 1988), p. 52.

[6] 'The Parthenon Sculptures: Facts and Figures', Clause 1.4.

[7] Select Committee Report, p. 47.

acquired by the British Museum in 1816 described above. Elgin claimed he had permission to take what he did from the Parthenon, but what about everything else he took from Greece (see Chapter 11)? Did Elgin have the necessary permissions to take everything in the Elgin Collection of Marbles?

CHAPTER 3

Elgin wants to sell. Should the Elgin Marbles be acquired for the nation?

Even in 1811, when Elgin first offered the Elgin Marbles to the British Museum, his action of taking them from the Parthenon was considered highly controversial.

The question of acquiring 'Lord Elgin's Marbles' first came before the House of Commons in June 1815.[1] Concern was expressed as to 'how Lord Elgin got possessed of the Marbles'. Sir John Newton told the House of Commons, 'He was afraid that the noble lord had ... committed the most flagrant acts of spoliation ... It was the duty of the House to ascertain the truth in these matters; for otherwise ... they would evidently sanction acts of public robbery.'[2] Spoil is plunder taken from the enemy in war; spoliation means the act of plundering. Plunder applies to what is taken not only in war but in robbery, grafting or swindling. There was no state of war between Britain and Turkey, which held Athens. Public robbery is a serious charge, and Newton's concerns were shared by others, both in and out of parliament. Spoliation is a word that recurs in discussions about the taking of the Elgin Marbles.

The question of acquiring the Elgin Marbles was next debated in the House of Commons in February 1816.[3] At the time, it was common for private individuals to travel from England to the Continent, where they acquired Greek and

---

[1] Petition of the Earl of Elgin respecting his Collection of Marbles, HC Deb, vol. 31, 15 June 1815, col. 828.

[2] Petition of the Earl of Elgin respecting his Collection of Marbles, HC Deb, vol. 31, 15 June 1815, col. 829.

[3] The Earl of Elgin's Petition respecting his Collection of Statues &c., HC Deb, 23 February 1816, vol. 32, col. 823.

Roman antiquities. However, in 1816 it was suggested in the House of Commons that if Elgin, a British ambassador, acquired the marbles while carrying out his public duties, then the marbles automatically belonged to the public. If the marbles belonged to the public, then they were not Elgin's to sell, and accordingly no payment should be made to him out of public funds for them. It was suggested instead that he should be reimbursed only his expenses for obtaining the marbles, not their true worth.

In the House of Commons debate, Member of Parliament (MP) Mr Preston made the point that if British ambassadors were encouraged to make these speculations, many might then return home in the character of merchants. The concern was that ambassadors would return to England laden with other countries' cultural treasures. Preston felt he could only agree to pay Elgin his expenses.

Lord Ossulston then asked 'whether an ambassador, residing in the territory of a foreign power, should have the right of appropriating to himself, and receiving benefits from objects belonging to that power'. This concern was widespread in the House of Commons. Mr Abercrombie MP responded that 'it was a matter of public duty not to hold out the precedent to ambassadors to avail themselves of their situation to obtain such property, and convert it to their own purposes'. Another MP, Mr Babington, 'thought it of great importance to ascertain whether this collection had been procured by such means as were honourable to this county'. Parliament wanted to know the precise manner in which Elgin 'got possessed of them'.

In order to satisfy the concerns expressed in parliament, a Select Committee of the House of Commons was appointed to consider the marbles under four principal heads:

- Elgin's authority by which the collection of marbles was acquired;
- the circumstances under which the authority was granted;
- the merit of the marbles as works of sculpture; and
- the value of the marbles.[4]

---

[4] Select Committee Report, p. 1.

CHAPTER 4

Private individual or British ambassador?

It is claimed today that Elgin was granted permission to take the marbles as a private individual, but this is not correct.

In 1815, the Select Committee considered the authority by which Elgin acquired the collection of marbles. The issue to be decided was: did Elgin obtain the marbles as a private individual, or was he only able to get them because he was Britain's ambassador in Turkey?

Athens was under Turkish control, so the permission of the Turkish government would have been needed. If it was found that Elgin obtained the marbles in his capacity as British ambassador then parliament would only pay him his expenses and not the actual value of the marbles. Elgin maintained he obtained the marbles as a private individual and offered to sell them at market value. But as will be explained in Chapter 19 he did not get it; parliament only agreed to pay Elgin his expenses.

The British Museum, in making its case to retain the marbles, claims that the Select Committee, after examining a number of witnesses, was of the opinion that Elgin had the permission of the Turkish authorities as a private individual.[1] However, this is factually wrong.

The Select Committee examined seventeen witnesses, three of whom were specifically questioned as to whether Elgin received the Turkish permission as a private individual or as Britain's ambassador. All three witnesses had been in Turkey; two of them spoke from personal experience of having obtained, or attempted to obtain, Turkish permissions to remove antiquities from Greece.

---

[1] 'The Parthenon Sculptures: Facts and Figures', Clause 9.2.4.

The first witness, Lord Aberdeen, said, 'I do not think a private individual could have accomplished the removal of the remains which Lord Elgin obtained', and he added, 'Therefore I conceive it certainly must have required very considerable influence not only with the Government [Turkish], but in the country [Greece], to be able to carry it into execution.'[2]

The second witness, John B. S. Morritt MP, a traveller and classical scholar, was questioned as to the capacity in which Elgin obtained the marbles. He said, 'When I was there [Athens] in 1796, I certainly conceived nothing but the influence of a public character could obtain that permission.'[3]

The third witness was Reverend Dr Philip Hunt, who went to Turkey as Elgin's chaplain and told the Select Committee he 'occasionally acted as [Elgin's] secretary'. When Hunt was asked, 'Do you think that any British subject, not in the situation of ambassador, would have been able to obtain from the Turkish Government a fermaun [permission] of such extensive powers?', he replied, 'Certainly not.'[4]

Henry Bankes, who chaired the Select Committee, stated in a subsequent debate in the House of Commons that 'with respect to the manner in which the Elgin Marbles had been acquired, the object certainly could not have been attained had Lord Elgin not been a British ambassador'.[5]

So in 1816 there was a consensus that Elgin only obtained the permission because he was Britain's ambassador, and not in any other capacity.

In 1916, one hundred years after the British Museum acquired the Elgin Marbles, there was still a consensus on this point. The British Museum agreed with the consensus, as evidenced by Smith, Keeper at the British Museum, who wrote in 1916 that the Select Committee agreed with Lord Aberdeen and Dr Hunt, that only an ambassador in his formal capacity would have obtained such extensive powers.[6]

---

[2] Select Committee Report, p. 49.

[3] Select Committee Report, p. 52.

[4] Select Committee Report, p. 57.

[5] Elgin Marbles, HC Deb, 7 June 1816, vol. 34, col. 1028.

[6] Smith, 'Lord Elgin and his Collection', p. 340.

However, the British Museum maintains today that in 1816 the Select Committee, after examining a series of witnesses, was of the opinion that Elgin had acted with permission as a private individual. This is factually wrong. The British Museum qualify what they say by adding, 'although it was suggested in 1816 that such permission might only have been given to an Ambassador'.[7] However, in 1816 no witness made any such suggestion. Every single witness, including those selected by Elgin to support his case before the Select Committee and the chairman (who was pro Elgin), was adamant that Elgin only obtained the permission because he was Britain's ambassador.

Today the British Museum is categorically wrong. However, in order to retain the sculptured marbles from the Parthenon the British Museum *must* maintain what it does. This is because if Elgin obtained the marbles as ambassador, then they did not belong to him. If Elgin never had title to the marbles, then it is impossible for the British Museum to have obtained title to the marbles from Elgin (see Chapter 28).

---

[7] 'The Parthenon Sculptures: Facts and Figures', Clause 9.2.4.

CHAPTER 5

A plunderer or a man of the European Enlightenment?

Another plank in the British Museum's case to retain the Elgin Marbles is that Elgin was a man of the European Enlightenment.[1]

The British Museum maintains that Elgin's actions must be judged according to the times he lived in and by the standards of his day.[2]

What Elgin did was never deemed acceptable, not even in his day. Elgin was judged exceedingly badly by the standards of his day.

---

[1] 'The Parthenon Sculptures: Facts and Figures', Clause 9.2.2.

[2] 'The Parthenon Sculptures: Facts and Figures', Clause 10.2.

CHAPTER 6

The Elgin Marbles Debate, 1816

In 1816, Elgin was savaged by members of parliament in the House of Commons for taking the marble sculptures from the Parthenon.

The Select Committee published its report on 18 March 1816. On 7 June, three months after its publication, the House of Commons debated as to whether the Elgin Marbles should be bought for the nation.[1] The debate is referred to here as the Marbles Debate. The Marbles Debate reveals how badly Elgin and his actions were judged by members of parliament in his own day.

Sir John Newton voted against the resolution 'on the ground of the unjustifiable nature by which the marbles were acquired'. A year earlier the same member had described what Elgin did as a 'flagrant act of spoliation'.

Mr Serjeant Best said that 'Lord Elgin had not acted as he ought to have done ... these Marbles had been brought to this country in breach of good faith.'

Another member, Lord Milton, 'could not agree that they had been acquired consistently with the strict rules of morality'.

Mr Croker 'could not consent to their purchase, lest by doing so he should render himself a partaker in the guilt of spoliation. He did not object to the bargain on the ground of economy, but of justice.'

Mr Hammersley voted against, 'on the ground of the dishonesty of the transaction ... it thus appeared that bribery had been employed ... it is regretted that the Government had not restrained this act of spoliation ... we should not place in

---

[1] Elgin Marbles, HC Deb, 7 June 1816, vol. 34, col. 1027.

our museum a monument of our disgrace.' He added, 'It thus appears that a British ambassador had taken advantage of our success over the French [in Egypt] to plunder the City of Athens.'

During the Marbles Debate only two members, out of the 112 members who voted on the motion, spoke in support of Elgin's actions. This is a damning statistic. It is also a true reflection of how Elgin was judged by the standards of his day.

Henry Bankes, one of the two members of parliament who supported Elgin's actions, misled parliament in the Marbles Debate. He told the House of Commons that no objections had been made in Athens when Elgin removed the marbles, and claimed that 'not only the local authorities of Athens were favourable'.[2] Bankes's assertion is untrue because as Chairman of the Select Committee he had asked a witness, John Morritt who had visited Athens, 'Do you think the Greeks were anxious that those Marbles should not be removed from Athens?' Morritt had replied, 'They were decidedly and strongly desirous that they should not be removed.'[3] Bankes was clearly biased in favour of Elgin and mislead parliament.

In 1816, parliament did not consider that Elgin was in any way enlightened, as the British Museum maintains today. Parliament was firmly of the view that Elgin's taking the marbles from the Parthenon was an appalling act.

Parliamentary debates spanning more than two hundred years are available online at Historic Hansard.[4] However, there are two years missing, one of which is 1816. A review of the debates in 1816 does not reveal any apparent reason why this year should not be online, unless it is a deliberate attempt to conceal the mauling that Elgin received in the House of Commons Marbles Debate on 7 June 1816.

It was not only in parliament that Elgin took a hammering. Lord Byron savaged Elgin in his poem *Childe Harold's Pilgrimage*, accusing him of being another Verres, a Roman magistrate who

---

[2] Elgin Marbles, HC Deb, 7 June 1816, vol. 34, col. 1028.

[3] Select Committee Report, p. 52.

[4] Historic Hansard (1803–2005). <hansard.millbanksystems.com/lords/>. Last accessed: 11 August 2016.

governed Sicily and was charged with stealing art from the island.

The British Museum's contention that Elgin's actions were acceptable in his own day is categorically not true.

CHAPTER 7

Who should have the Elgin Marbles: Britain, France, Greece or Russia?

In making its case to keep the Elgin Marbles, the British Museum states that requests for the removal of the marbles from the museum are not new, and that the idea was first mooted by Hugh Hammersley MP in the Marbles Debate in 1816.[1] However, Hammersley did not propose that the marbles should be removed from the British Museum; he could not have made any such proposal, because when the Marbles Debate took place the marbles were *not* in the British Museum. What Hammersley actually suggested was more radical.

In 1816, Hammersley proposed the following amendment to the motion in the Marbles Debate:

> ... having taken into consideration the manner in which the Earl of Elgin became possessed of certain ancient sculptured marbles from Athens ... that Great Britain holds these marbles only in trust till they are demanded by the present, *or any future,* possessors of the city of Athens; and upon such demand, engages without question or negotiation, to restore them, as far as can be effected, to the places from where they were taken, and that they shall be in the mean time carefully preserved in the British Museum [emphasis added].[2]

Hammersley made a powerful case, but shot himself in the foot. His words 'or any future possessors of the city of Athens', were a death knell for his proposed amendment. Mr Croker, a member

[1] 'The Parthenon Sculptures: Facts and Figures', Clause 7.1.

[2] Elgin Marbles, HC Deb, 7 June 1816, vol. 34, col. 1032.

of the Select Committee, described Hammersley's proposed amendment as farcical. Croker told the House of Commons that Russia would be next to take Greece from Turkey, and that it was absurd that Britain should hold the marbles in trust until such time as Russia took Athens and demanded the marbles from Britain. 'Spoliation must precede the attainment of them by Russia', he said. Croker acknowledged there was spoliation and succeeded in making a case in favour of it.

Bankes, the Chairman of the Select Committee who misled parliament, told the House of Commons that 'the greatest desire, too, had been evinced by the government of France to become possessed of them [the marbles]'. This is correct; a few pieces of the sculptured marbles from the Parthenon were, and still are, in the Louvre. France coveted more pieces from the Parthenon.

In the early 1800s, Britain and France were competing with each other for antiquities from the eastern Mediterranean. In 1802, the French got their hands on the Rosetta Stone, but British soldiers took it from the French in Egypt before it could be transported to France. Much as parliament abhorred what Elgin had done, the thought of the Elgin Marbles being in the possession of the French, defeated at the Battle of Waterloo twelve months earlier, was extremely unpalatable.

Despite the mauling Elgin received in the Marbles Debate, the House of Commons voted in favour of the original motion to grant £35,000 to the British Museum to acquire the marbles. The vote was eighty-two for, thirty against.

If it had not been for the prospect of the marbles going to Russia or France, the House of Commons would have voted for the amendment that the British Museum preserve the marbles in trust until they could be restored to Athens. If Hammersley's amendment had omitted the words 'or any future possessors of the city of Athens', and had been confined to holding the marbles in trust for the Greeks, then the Elgin Marbles would, without any shadow of a doubt, have been returned to Greece a long time ago.

Postscript: 'Who should have the Elgin Marbles … Russia?'

Russia never took Greece from Turkey, but they did get one of the Parthenon marbles – on a short-term loan.

In 2014, the British Museum made a clandestine loan of one of the Elgin Marbles to Russia. *The Times* published a front page world exclusive under the heading 'Elgin Marbles moved out of Britain for first time: Secret journey to Russia of Greek masterpiece'.[3] *The Times* devoted the entire front page, a further five pages and a leading article to the loan to Russia.

Greece refuses to recognise the British Museum's ownership of the Elgin Marbles. The secret loan of one of the Parthenon Sculptures by the British Museum to Russia caused outrage in Greece.[4] The outrage of Greece's prime minister, Antonis Samaras, in 2014 sits well with the outrage of the members of parliament in 1816 who were against Elgin taking the marbles from the Parthenon.

---

[3] Jack Malvern and Ben Hoyle, 'Elgin Marbles moved out of Britain for first time', *The Times*, 5 December 2014, p. 1.

[4] Jack Malvern and Ben Hoyle, 'Greece slams UK for loan of statue', *The Times*, 6 December 2014, p. 1.

Chapter 8

The sculptures for free

Elgin paid nothing for the Parthenon Sculptures. He did not even pay one pound.

In Elgin's expenses, submitted to the Select Committee of the House of Commons, there is no purchase price for the Elgin Marbles. The fact that Elgin did not pay for the marbles is one of the single most important facts relating to the Elgin Marbles Debate, yet it is not included in the British Museum's 'The Parthenon Sculptures: Facts and Figures'. However, the British Museum does acknowledge elsewhere that Elgin did not pay for them, stating that it is a popular misconception that Elgin purchased the Elgin Marbles.[1]

It will come as a surprise to generations of commentators in Britain and America that Elgin did not pay anything for the marbles. Many letter writers, historians and journalists have vehemently opposed the return of the Elgin Marbles to Greece on the grounds that Elgin bought the marbles, stressing he paid for them with his own money. Hundreds upon hundreds of letters to newspapers, and articles written over two centuries, all based on a false premise, have served the case – that the British Museum should retain the Elgin Marbles – exceedingly well.

In stating that Elgin did not buy the marbles, the British Museum maintains that the permission to take the marbles was granted to Elgin by the Turkish authorities as a personal gesture, and that this gesture was made after Elgin encouraged British forces in their fight to drive French forces out of Egypt,

---

[1] 'The Parthenon Sculptures.' *The British Museum.* <www.britishmuseum.org/about_us/news_and_press/statements/parthenon_sculptures.aspx>. Last accessed: 27 July 2016.

which at the time was under Turkish control.[2] However, Elgin was Britain's ambassador in Constantinople; he was not a politician or a military officer. He would have had little direct influence over British forces, whether in Egypt or elsewhere.

In 1816, the Select Committee obtained a valuation of £60,800 (£42.2 million in current values) for the 249 pieces that made up the Elgin Collection of Marbles. The assertion that Turkish authorities would have permitted Elgin to take such a valuable collection without either payment or bribery is absurd.

---

[2] 'The Parthenon Sculptures.' *The British Museum.* <www.britishmuseum.org/about_us/news_and_press/statements/parthenon_sculptures.aspx>. Last accessed: 27 July 2016.

CHAPTER 9

'At a great expense' and the bankruptcy myth

It is claimed that Elgin spent so much of his own money to get the marbles that he bankrupted himself. This is a myth.

In 2014 *The Times*, in a leading article, called for the Elgin Marbles to remain at the British Museum and claimed that Elgin had collected the marbles at some personal cost.[1] This, too, is a myth.

The consensus today is that Elgin incurred personal costs and that in acquiring the marbles he bankrupted himself. This claim is repeatedly made when stating the case to retain the Elgin Marbles in the British Museum. However, Elgin did not pay anything for the marbles; the cost of obtaining them was not funded from his own resources but entirely by the British government (see Chapter 16).

In 1816, parliament passed An Act to vest the Elgin Collection of ancient Marbles and Sculpture in the Trustees of the British Museum for the Use of the Public. The recital (the preamble) to the Act of Parliament states that Elgin had 'at a great expense made a most valuable collection of ancient marbles and sculpture'. However, this is not true, and the government knew this to be untrue in 1816 because it provided Elgin with the entire funds to obtain the marbles.

In 1963, the then current Lord Elgin sent a memorandum to Prime Minister Harold Macmillan in which he stated that Elgin's cost in obtaining the marbles was £90,000 as at 1803.[2] This memorandum was forwarded to the Earl of Dundee, the Minister of State for Foreign Affairs, who in a parliamentary

---

[1] 'No Losing the marbles: The Parthenon sculptures should remain at the British Museum', *The Times* 14 October 2014, p. 30.

[2] Background papers to British Museum Act 1963, NA, T 218/549.

debate on the British Museum Bill 1963 said, 'I believe it cost the great-grandfather of the present Lord Elgin £90,000'.[3]

However, Elgin himself, in his submission to the Select Committee of the House of Commons, had no purchase price, but put his total expenditure 'prior to 1803 ... at £28,000'. To this he added £5,000, and then fourteen years' interest totalling £23,240.[4] But the £28,000 Elgin spent on obtaining the marbles was entirely funded by the British government, and the government did not claim any interest from Elgin.

Obtaining the marbles did not bankrupt Elgin. In fact, he made a profit on the marbles (see Chapter 17). He did not pay anything for the marbles, and his financial difficulties were wholly unrelated to his removal of the marbles from the Parthenon.

---

[3] British Museum Bill, HL Deb, 9 April 1963, vol. 248, col. 963.

[4] Select Committee Report, Appendix 6, p. 67.

CHAPTER 10

Bribing Turkish authorities … in Turkey

It is vigorously claimed that Elgin did not pay bribes in order to obtain the Elgin Marbles – but it can be established, beyond any doubt, that he did.

One of the witnesses called to give evidence to the Select Committee was John B. S. Morritt MP. He was firmly of the view that Elgin only received permission from the Turkish government because he was Britain's ambassador. He also asserted that the Greeks 'were decidedly and strongly desirous that they [the marbles] should not be removed'.[1]

Morritt was called as a witness because he had visited the Parthenon in 1795.[2] He was an expert witness on two counts: the first was to the physical state of the Parthenon five years before Elgin removed the sculptures; the second was to the attitude of the Turkish government to the removal of sculptures from the Parthenon. Morritt had first-hand experience of this because he himself tried to take sculptures from the Parthenon. He admitted to the Select Committee that he had bribed local officials in his attempt to take marbles.

Morritt was asked, 'Was there in the Turkish government and people a desire of preserving these remains, or did they seem careless about their being broken to pieces and pulled down?' Morritt replied, 'When I was there, the Turkish government totally neglected the care of such Marbles as were loose or thrown down, but certainly interfered to prevent any Marbles from being removed which were standing and in their places.'[3] Morritt went on:

---

[1] Select Committee Report, p. 52.

[2] At the time he was not a Member of Parliament.

[3] Select Committee Report, p. 52.

> It was generally understood that the [Turkish] Government wished to prevent anything from being removed, that the local [Turkish] governors of Athens, who were assailable by bribery, endeavoured to conduct the business as secretly as they could, whenever any thing was to be removed, even of the Marbles which were down. I myself negotiated with the commander of the citadel [the Parthenon] for the removal of one or two pieces of the frieze, that were thrown down and neglected among rubbish: he was very willing to do it for a sum of money, if he could do it without the knowledge of any person whatsoever.[4]

Morritt added that nothing came of his negotiations with the Turkish official in Athens.

The Select Committee wanted further clarification on the Turkish government's stance regarding pieces of sculpture that had *not* fallen to the ground and asked Morritt, 'You understood there was always a great difference between the Marbles already down, and those that were standing in their places?' Morritt replied:

> I had endeavoured to include in the bargain [with the corrupt official] one of the metopes which had not fallen ... I found him much more scrupulous on this point than with respect to those that had fallen; and I think that he would not do so on any consideration [bribe] have allowed those that were secure to be removed.[5]

When Elgin's workmen hacked sculptures from the Parthenon it was already damaged. However, it was not an abandoned ruin, as is frequently claimed. Four years before Elgin commenced his operations to remove marbles Morritt visited the Parthenon, writing, 'In the middle of this fine building the Turks have built a small shabby mosque.'[6]

Morritt was candid before the Select Committee about bribing officials, but at the same time, he was less than frank

---

[4] Select Committee Report, p. 52.

[5] Select Committee Report, p. 52.

[6] John B. S. Morritt, *The Letters of John B. S. Morritt of Rokeby: Descriptive of Journeys in Europe and Asia Minor in the Years 1794–1796* (London: John Murray, 1914), p. 174.

regarding what he hoped to take from the Parthenon. In a letter written while he was in Athens, Morritt discussed fifteen metopes that remained fixed on the Parthenon: 'They represent the combat of the Centaurs and Lapithae ... we have just breakfasted, and are meditating a walk to the citadel [Parthenon], where our Greek attendant is gone to meet the workmen, and is, I hope, hammering down the Centaurs and Lapithae.'[7]

Morritt's workmen did not hammer down the metopes, but Elgin's workmen did. The notion that Elgin mainly took pieces of sculpture that had fallen to the ground is a myth. In his written submissions to the Select Committee, Elgin stated that he employed six artists for three and a half years to make drawings of the sculptured marbles on the Parthenon.[8] Giovanni Battista Lusieri, an Italian painter, and five other artists were not employed for three and a half years to draw pieces of marble scattered on the ground. They drew the frieze and metopes on the Parthenon, and it took them years to do so. The sculptures were then removed by Elgin and shipped to England.

An incident that occurred over a century before Elgin took the marbles is persistently put forward as a justification for Elgin taking them. In 1687, the Parthenon and some of the sculptures were damaged when a Turkish ammunition store inside the building exploded during the Venetian siege of the Acropolis.[9] This isolated incident, and the claims that occupying Turkish forces were using the marbles for target practice, make Elgin appear to be the rescuer of the marbles. However, the claims are not true. None of the marbles in the British Museum or in the new Acropolis Museum in Athens have any ballistic damage. Evidence of the condition of the Parthenon, and of the marbles when Elgin took them, can be found in the remarkable drawings made by Elgin's artists, published in Luciana Gallo's book, *Lord Elgin and Ancient Greek Architecture: The Elgin Drawings*

---

[7] Morritt, *The Letters of John B. S. Morritt of Rokeby*, p. 180.

[8] Select Committee Report, p. 64.

[9] The siege lasted six days, 23–29 September 1687, during the Morean War (Sixth Ottoman–Venetian War, 1684–1699).

at the British Museum, which includes drawings published for the first time in 2009.[10]

Elgin's workmen hacked sculptures from the Parthenon and it was a massive operation. In his evidence to the Select Committee, Elgin said, 'I employed three to four hundred people a day.'[11] Fourteen of the fifteen metopes, which Morritt saw on the Parthenon, with the Centaurs and Lapithae, form part of the Elgin Collection of Marbles and are listed in Appendix 11 (Section B) of the Select Committee Report.[12]

An English traveller who was in Athens wrote a first-hand eyewitness account of the metopes being taken down by Elgin's workmen and of the damage done to the Parthenon.

> Our guide began by showing us the Parthenon ... Some workmen, employed under the directions of the British Ambassador [Elgin] were engaged in making preparations, by means of ropes and pulleys for taking down the metopes, where the sculpture *remained most perfect*. When it was being removed a part of the adjoining masonry was loosened by the machinery; and down came the fine masses of Petelican marble, scattering their white fragments with thundering noise among the ruins [emphasis added].[13]

In the 1816 Marbles Debate, Hammersley stated that 'it thus appeared that bribery had been employed [by Elgin]'. In 1815, Lord Aberdeen gave evidence to the Select Committee, but he did not use the word bribery. Instead, he claimed that for Elgin to obtain the permission it may have been 'necessary to conciliate those authorities by means of presents'.[14]

There is an important distinction between giving presents and payments being 'necessary'. There is also an important distinction between payments being necessary in Athens and

---

[10] Luciana Gallo, *Lord Elgin and Ancient Greek Architecture: The Elgin Drawings at the British Museum* (Cambridge: Cambridge University Press, 2009).

[11] Select Committee Report, p. 19.

[12] Select Committee Report, p.71.

[13] Edward D. Clarke, *Travels in Various Countries of Europe, Asia and Africa. Part 2: Greece, Egypt and the Holy Land* (London: T. Cadell and W. Davies, 1814), p. 483.

[14] Select Committee Report, p. 49.

payments being necessary in Turkey. In Athens, inducements would have been necessary to physically remove the marbles. However, if payments had been made in Turkey they would have been in order to obtain the permission to remove the marbles, as Athens was under the control of the Turkish government.

Elgin did make presents in Athens – to the Turkish authorities in Athens. Elgin records these in his expenses as 'Presents, found *necessary* for the local authorities, in Athens *alone* – Piastres 21,902' [emphasis added].[15] The phrase 'in Athens alone' implies they were also made elsewhere.

The British Museum corrects another of the 'Further common misconceptions', this one specifically relating to bribery. It maintains that presents were given by Elgin to Turkish officials in Athens according to the custom of the time, but that those presents did not amount to £600.[16] The historian William St Clair, who had access to Elgin's papers, wrote that presents to the authorities in Athens between 1803 and 1815 amounted to over £6,000 (£4.16 million in current values) – ten times the amount claimed by the British Museum.[17]

There has never been a time, in any country, when ambassadors did not give presents.[18] However, in Elgin's time, bribery was endemic in Greece and Turkey, as the following story illustrates.

In 1815, John Fazakerley MP gave evidence to the Select Committee that was looking into how Elgin obtained the Parthenon Sculptures. Fazakerley was in Athens in 1810 and 1811, immediately before the removal of the Aegina Marbles, another group of important sculptures removed from Greece which, as with the Elgin Marbles, the Greek government want returned to Greece.

Fazakerley was asked, 'Was there great difficulty in removing them [the Aegina Marbles] out of Greece?' Fazakerley replied, 'Certainly, very great.' Fazakerley told the Select Committee that he was asked by Mr Cockerell to consult the British Consul on

---

[15] Select Committee Report, Appendix 5, p. 66.

[16] 'The Parthenon Sculptures: Facts and Figures', Clause 9.3.

[17] St Clair, *Lord Elgin and the Marbles*, p. 252.

[18] Gifts to the British government are officially recorded.

the subject.[19] 'The Consul told me he felt great embarrassment on the subject, and that they must be removed either in secret or by bribery,' said Fazakerley. This extraordinary advice from the British Consul relating to the removal of the Aegina Marbles from Greece is on record in the Select Committee Report.[20]

Fazakerley told the Select Committee that the Aegina Marbles belonged to four individuals: two Englishmen, Mr Cockerell and Mr Foster, and two Germans who he did not name.[21] In 1811, the British Museum sent a representative to Malta, to where the Aegina Marbles had been spirited, in an unsuccessful attempt to buy them. The Aegina Marbles were acquired by the Prince of Bavaria and today are in the Glyptothek Museum in Munich, Germany.

Secrecy or bribery were the only options available to anyone looking to remove antiquities from Turkish controlled Greece.

The sculptured marbles from the Parthenon were clearly too bulky to be taken secretly, so Elgin not only gave presents in Athens, but also paid bribes in Turkey. These payments are recorded in Elgin's expenses, which he presented to the Select Committee. However, they were not recorded as presents but, in Elgin's own words, to pay Turkish officials: 'Commission and Agency; which in all instances, especially when out of the ordinary line of business are very considerable *in Turkey*' [emphasis added].[22]

The amount – the quantum – of the bribes paid in Turkey has been deleted from Elgin's expenses, published as Appendix 5 of the Select Committee Report. Two other amounts have also been deleted so that the amount of the bribes cannot be deduced. However, given that Elgin states that the commission and agency payments in Turkey were 'very considerable', then the amount deleted from his expenses must also be 'very considerable'.

---

[19] Charles Robert Cockerell (1788–1863), an English architect and one of four owners of the Aegina Marbles.

[20] Select Committee Report, p. 54.

[21] The Germans were Baron Otto Magnus von Stackelberg (1786–1837) and Baron Carl Haller von Hallerstein (1774–1817).

[22] Select Committee Report, Appendix 5, p. 65.

It has been suggested that Elgin intentionally left the three amounts blank for the government to fill in, in the hope that the government would round up Elgin's expenses from £62,440 to £70,000.[23] Why should Elgin have imagined that the government would make up expenses on his behalf? But let us assume for a moment that Elgin did leave the three amounts blank. One of the blanks relates to 'Commission and Agency; which in all instances, especially when out of the ordinary line of business are very considerable in Turkey'.[24] How can Elgin have imagined the British government would fill in this blank on his behalf? The answer is that the government did not, because the amount was not left blank. Who would submit an account with seven items of expenditure and leave three of the seven items blank? Who would believe that if there were three blanks in Elgin's expense accounts it would have gone unnoted by the Select Committee?

In 1816, Nicholas Vansittart, the Chancellor of the Exchequer, played a significant role in securing the marbles. He told the House of Commons that 'the [Select] committee to be appointed would of course consider the question of the expenses of the noble Lord *carefully* and see also whether they had been properly applied or not' [emphasis added].[25] If there had been any blanks in Elgin's expenses submitted to the Select Committee then Elgin would have been asked why there were blanks. Given that the Select Committee considered the expenses 'carefully' and examined Elgin over two days but did not query any blanks, this establishes that the blanks were not in Elgin's submissions to the Select Committee, but only in the Select Committee Report made available to the public.

Elgin's expenses recording the commission and agency payments made in Turkey were first prepared in 1811.[26] Then in 1816, Elgin submitted revised accounts of his expenses relating to the marbles.[27]

---

[23] St Clair, *Lord Elgin and the Marbles*, p. 185.

[24] Select Committee Report, Appendix 5, p. 65.

[25] The Earl of Elgin's Petition, HC Deb, 23 February 1816, vol. 32, col. 828.

[26] Select Committee Report, Appendix 5, p. 63.

[27] Select Committee Report, Appendix 6, p. 66.

The differences between the two sets of accounts are interesting. In the 1811 expenses appears the line, 'Commission and Agency; which in all instances, especially when out of the ordinary line of business are very considerable in Turkey.'[28] However, in 1816 that line has disappeared in his revised accounts. The amount of commission and agency in Turkey is subsumed with labour and/or interest charges. There has been a deliberate attempt to conceal the fact that Elgin paid bribes in Turkey.

Today, the British Museum maintains that Elgin gave presents in Athens, but it is silent about any payments in Turkey. However, in 1916 Smith, Keeper of Greek and Roman Antiquities at the British Museum, wrote that Elgin explained that all privileges in *Turkey* had to be paid for on a scale proportioned to the rank of parties and the eagerness shown for the acquisition.[29] There is no point in mincing words, as Smith did: Elgin paid bribes in Turkey and, as Elgin clearly stated in his 1811 expense accounts, the payments were 'very considerable'.

In the 1816 Marbles Debate, Mr Serjeant Best maintained that 'the firman [permission] could do nothing without bribery'.[30] The presents, which Elgin said were necessary for the local authorities in Athens, were made to enable scaffolding to be erected around the Parthenon (the scaffolding had previously been resisted). The scaffolding was necessary to hack marbles from the edifice of the Parthenon. Elgin confirmed to the Select Committee that, for nine months from August 1800, his team had only been permitted to make drawings of the marbles but not to remove anything. Elgin further confirmed that it was not until April 1801 that they received permission to put up scaffolding.

The fact that Elgin paid bribes in Turkey and was not permitted to remove the marbles as a personal favour granted to him by the Turkish government fundamentally alters the two

---

[28] Select Committee Report, Appendix 5, p. 65.

[29] Smith, 'Lord Elgin and his Collection', p. 310.

[30] Elgin Marbles, HC Deb, 7 June 1816, vol. 34, col. 1037.

hundred-year Elgin Marbles Debate. Contrary to what the British Museum maintains, the manner in which Elgin obtained the Elgin Marbles can be challenged.

CHAPTER 11

Elgin in Athens

It is widely believed that Elgin was in Turkey when marble sculptures were hacked from the Parthenon and packed and shipped to England. However, Elgin was in Athens twice when his workmen removed sculptures, a fact he did not disclose in his evidence to the Select Committee of the House of Commons in 1816.

Elgin was appointed ambassador at Constantinople on 14 August 1799.[1] He arrived to take up his post on 6 November 1799, travelling onboard HMS *Phaeton*,[2] and left Constantinople on 16 January 1803 onboard HMS *Diana*.[3] However, he did not remain in Constantinople throughout his three-and-a-half-year appointment.

In 1802, in an unusual move, Elgin officially relinquished his duties as ambassador for five months in order to go to Athens. He put Alexander Straton in charge of the embassy in Constantinople. Straton's correspondence with the Foreign Office during Elgin's absence, from 31 March 1802 to 3 September 1802, is at the National Archives.

On the 31 March 1802, Straton wrote to Lord Hawkesbury, the Foreign Secretary (replacing Lord Grenville), to inform him 'that Lord Elgin set out for Athens the day before yesterday after having officially announced to the Porte [Turkish

---

[1] Turkey: Letters and Papers from the Earl of Elgin at Constantinople, to the Secretary of State: with Drafts to him. From August 14, 1799 to December 31, 1799, NA, FO 78/24, p. 2.

[2] HMS *Phaeton*, Master's Logs, 20 July 1799 to 26 February 1802, NA, ADM 52/3285.

[3] Turkey: Letters and Papers from Mr. Straton at Constantinople and Buyukdere to the Secretary of State from January 25, 1803 to May 10, 1803, NA, FO 78/39, p. 3.

government] and to the foreign ministers residing here that I was to be charged with the business of this Embassy during His Excellency's absence'.[4] Elgin did not return to Constantinople until 8 September 1802.[5]

In 1816, the Select Committee sought to establish exactly what took place in Athens, as this was pertinent to how Elgin got the sculptures from the Parthenon. The Select Committee called a number of witnesses who had been in Athens. The opening question put to four of these witnesses was, 'In what year were you at Athens?'[6] Elgin's chaplain and secretary, Dr Philip Hunt, was questioned at length as to what he did in Athens; yet in contrast Elgin himself was not asked if he had been in Athens. He was the only witness to have been in Athens but not asked about it.

Elgin was first asked 'to state the circumstances under which [he] became possessed of this Collection'.[7] Elgin was questioned over two days, yet at no stage did he volunteer that he had been in Athens twice when his workmen removed marble sculptures from the Parthenon.

Members of the Select Committee were fully aware that Elgin had been in Athens. Nicholas Vansittart, a member of the Select Committee and Chancellor of the Exchequer, funded through the Treasury Straton's tenure in Constantinople during Elgin's official five month absence, so he clearly knew.

Elgin was asked by Bankes, the Chairman of the Select Committee, whether the permission he received was 'to take particular pieces, one from the city and one from the citadel [Parthenon] and so on?' Elgin replied, 'No; I had never been at Athens, and could not specify any thing.'[8] However, after the permission was granted Elgin did go to Athens and personally selected the Greek antiquities to ship to England.

---

[4] Turkey: Letters and Papers from Mr. Alexander Straton (chargé d'affaires during the Earl of Elgin's absence) at Constantinople, to the Secretary of State: with Drafts. From March 31, 1802 to September 3, 1802, NA, FO 78/37.

[5] Checkland, *The Elgins, 1788–1917*, p. 56.

[6] The four witnesses were John B. S. Morritt, John Fazakerley, the Earl of Aberdeen and William Wilkins, an architect.

[7] Select Committee Report, p. 17.

[8] Select Committee Report, p. 23.

Elgin's hands-on procurement of antiquities in Athens is described in the *Memorandum on the Subject of the Earl of Elgin's Pursuits in Greece* (1810).[9] The following are some of the antiquities Elgin took and their present whereabouts:

- A tumulus (believed to be the tomb of Aspasia) that was excavated 'under Lord Elgin's eye during his residence at Athens'. From this tomb Elgin took 'a large marble vase, five feet in circumference, inclosing one of bronze thirteen inches in diameter'.[10] On the day before the tumulus was excavated Elgin wrote to Lusieri, 'The people of the [HMS] *Diana* ought to be at the Piraeus [Athens's port] at dawn, for the excavation of the tumulus.'[11] This marble vase, an urn, formed part of Elgin's collection acquired by the British Museum in 1816.[12]
- 'Permission was obtained from the archbishop of Athens, to examine the interior of all churches and convents in Athens and its neighbourhood, in search of antiquities, and his authority was frequently employed to permit Lord Elgin to appropriate any curious fragment of antiquity ... This search furnished ... a Gymnasiarch's chair in marble, on the back of which are figures of Harmodius and Aristogiton, with daggers in their hands, and the death of Leæna.'[13] The Gymnasiarch was the Director of Public Amusements and sat in the marble chair during the Athenian games. This chair is at Broomhall.[14] The chair was photographed there. Harmodius and Aristogiton became known as the Tyrannicides and are cited in photograph captions.[15]

---

9 *Memorandum on the Subject of the Earl of Elgin's Pursuits in Greece* (Edinburgh: Balfour, Kirkwood, & Co., 1810). Hereafter *Memorandum.*

10 *Memorandum,* p.19.

11 Smith, 'Lord Elgin and his Collection', p. 253.

12 Select Committee Report, p. 73, N12.

13 *Memorandum,* p. 20.

14 Smith, 'Lord Elgin and his Collection', pp. 286 and 294.

15 Charles Seltman, 'Two Athenian Marble Thrones', *Journal of Hellenic Studies,* 67 (November 1947), pp. 22–30.

- 'From the Theatre of Bacchus [at the foot of the Acropolis], Lord Elgin obtained the very ancient sun-dial, which existed there during the time of Aeschyles, Sophocles and Euripides and a large statue of Bacchus.'[16] The sun-dial and statue of Bacchus formed part of Elgin's collection acquired by the British Museum in 1816.[17]

The *Memorandum* describes other antiquities Elgin obtained in Athens, but it would be impossible to describe them all. The database of the British Museum Online Collection lists 562 objects as purchased from Thomas Bruce, 7th Earl of Elgin, 180 of which have the provenance 'from Athens'. The 562 objects do not include the Parthenon Sculptures. When individual pieces of sculpture and drawings are included, the total number of objects purchased from Elgin is 688.[18]

The overwhelming majority of the 688 objects were taken by Elgin from Greece (Athens, Aeginae, Argos, Attica, Corinth, Daphne, Delos, Epidaurus, Mycenae and Thebes). From Mycenae, Elgin took 'Ornamental sculptures, from the tomb of Agamemnon'.[19] Four of Elgin's objects from the tomb of Agamemnon (also called the Treasury of Atreus) are in the British Museum.[20]

Elgin went to Athens twice and was proactive in taking not only the Parthenon Sculptures but also the hundreds of Greek antiquities sold to the British Museum.

He was in Athens in 1802 to select and pack the contents of the cases that arrived in England that year. In August 1802, the *Exeter Flying Post* reported, 'This day fifteen cases of curious antique figures were landed [at Plymouth] from [HMS] *Diane* … these curiosities were collected by Lord Elgin Ambassador at

---

[16] *Memorandum*, p. 19.

[17] Select Committee Report, p. 73, K1 and K2.

[18] 'British Museum Online Collection.' *The British Museum*. <www.britishmuseum.org/research/collection_online/search.aspx> Last accessed: 21 July 2016.

[19] *Catalogue of the Antiquities in the Earl of Elgin's Museum* (London: Reynell printed for private circulation, 1815), Cat. no. 34.

[20] British Museum registration numbers 1816,0610.177; 1816,0610.180; 1816,0610.204; 1816,0610.224.

Constantinople chiefly in and about the ruins of Corinth and Athens.'[21] HMS *Diane* and HMS *Diana* (mentioned earlier) were two different ships. During his stay in Athens Elgin made excursions, including to Corinth. The excursions are mentioned in Elgin's and Lady Elgin's letters sent from Greece.[22]

Vansittart and others on the Select Committee clearly decided that Elgin's presence in Athens should form no part of their report to the House of Commons. This is because the Select Committee was appointed to enquire whether the Elgin Marbles had been properly acquired.

Vansittart clearly wanted the British Museum to have the Elgin Marbles. Before the Select Committee was appointed, on Vansittart's recommendation, Mr Rose claimed in the House of Commons that the trustees of the British Museum 'were determined to receive' the Elgin Marbles.[23] Vansittart was a trustee of the British Museum.

There is a consensus among historians and Elgin's biographers that Lusieri, one of the six artists employed by Elgin to make drawings and casts of the sculptures, was responsible for removing and shipping the sculptures to England. Lusieri is alleged to have done this while Elgin was in Constantinople. However, Elgin was in Athens, and Lusieri was not responsible for removing and shipping the sculptures (see Chapter 14).

Elgin's appointment as ambassador in Constantinople came to an end in January 1803. He went straight to Athens. He remained there for eight days, taking antiquities, excavating the tumulus and supervising the removal of part of the frieze of the Parthenon. From Athens he went to Naples, and then overland to Paris via Rome.[24]

---

[21] 'Plymouth', *Exeter Flying Post*, 19 August 1802, p. 4.

[22] Smith, 'Lord Elgin and his Collection', pp. 210–11.

[23] Petition of the Earl of Elgin respecting his Collection of Marbles, HC Deb, 15 June 1815, vol. 31, col. 830.

[24] HMS *Diana* Captain's Log records: 'loading Elgin's luggage in Constantinople, 16 January 1803; arriving Gulf of Athens, 27 January; sailing 3 February; arriving Malta 11 March with Elgin on board; taking Elgin to Naples' (NA, ADM 51/1447).

Elgin told the Select Committee that while in Paris 'I received a letter from an English traveller, complaining of Lusieri's taking down part of the frieze of the Parthenon'.[25] Lusieri was employed by Elgin and has become a convenient scapegoat.

[25] Select Committee Report, p. 21.

CHAPTER 12

A British Under-Secretary of State in Athens

The Select Committee called as a witness William Hamilton, Under-Secretary of State at the Foreign Office,[1] and asked him, 'Were you present at Athens during the removal of any part of the Marbles?' Hamilton replied, 'Yes, I was.' He was then asked, 'During the removal of those that were taken from the Parthenon?' He replied, 'Yes, I was.'[2]

So the second-highest-ranking official at the Foreign Office was in Athens when sculptures were hacked from the Parthenon. But Hamilton then added, 'I had nothing to do with them myself, being at Athens quite as a private individual.'3 The Select Committee accepted Hamilton's claim that he was in Athens as a private individual and had nothing to do with the Elgin Marbles. Yet it was not true. Hamilton was very much involved.

Hamilton, at the Foreign Office, instructed the Admiralty to send a ship to Athens to fetch the Elgin Marbles. The Admiralty recorded: 'Letter from Mr. Hamilton requesting that a Transport may be dispatched to Athens from Malta, to bring home a part of the valuable antiquities collected in Greece during the last 9 years by the Earl of Elgin.'[4]

Furthermore, Hamilton was the 'go-to' man at the Foreign Office when it came to getting the Elgin Marbles. This is evidenced by the Admiralty entry: 'the remainder of the Earl of Elgin's antiquities from Athens have been landed on that island [Malta] from the [HMS] *Hydra Transport.* Mr. Hamilton informed.'[5]

---

[1] *The Royal Kalendar* (London: J. Debrett, 1815), p. 147.

[2] Select Committee Report, p. 26.

[3] Select Committee Report, p. 26.

[4] Case 72.6, Freightage of Treasure, Admiralty Digest, 1809–1810, NA, ADM 12/144.

[5] Case 72.6, Freightage of Treasure, Admiralty Digest, 1809–1810, NA, ADM 12/147.

The contention in this book is that the British government financed the entire operation of obtaining the Elgin Marbles. It would be logical that someone from the government would attend in Athens to monitor operations. That person was the Under-Secretary of State at the Foreign Office, William Hamilton.

The Select Committee asked Hamilton whether the government had assisted Elgin in any way. Despite his hands-on role at the Foreign Office, where he directed the Admiralty to transport the sculptures, Hamilton denied that the government assisted Elgin in any way. What Hamilton maintained was clearly wanting and inadequate (see Chapter 21). What he said would never have been accepted by a parliamentary Select Committee intent on establishing the truth about how the Elgin Marbles had been taken from Athens.

Hamilton's entry in the *Oxford Dictionary of National Biography* states that in 1803 'he was found a place at the Foreign Office as a private secretary'.[6] He was appointed Under-Secretary in 1809. It is claimed here that Elgin arranged for Hamilton to be placed at the Foreign Office specifically to make transport arrangements with the Admiralty. The 'go-to' man at the Foreign Office was Elgin's man.

If this is far-fetched, consider that Hamilton:

- went to Constantinople with Elgin in 1799 as his attaché, becoming his personal secretary in 1802;
- was sent by Elgin to Rome and Naples to find artists to draw the Parthenon Sculptures. He returned to Constantinople with a draughtsman for drawing figures, two architectural draughtsmen and two cast-makers;[7]
- compiled an unpublished list of expenditure in Italy from October 1799 to April 1800 in procuring the artists;[8]
- on Elgin's instructions went to Athens in 1800 and, with the assistance of the British Consul, secured access for the artists to the Acropolis;[9]

---

[6] *Oxford Dictionary of National Biography* (*ODNB*) <www.oxforddnb.com/>. Last accessed: 12 August 2016.

[7] David M. Wilson, *The British Museum – A History* (London: The British Museum Press, 2002), p. 72.

[8] Gallo, *Lord Elgin and Ancient Greek Architecture*, p. 40.

[9] Gallo, *Lord Elgin and Ancient Greek Architecture*, p. 59.

- was in Athens again in 1802, from where he corresponded with Elgin;[10]
- was sent by Elgin to Egypt where he had a hands-on role in physically taking the Rosetta Stone, now in the British Museum, from the French;[11]
- purchased Arab horses for Elgin's stud at Broomhall.[12] HMS *Diana*'s log book has an entry for 'Naples 15 March 1803', 'Loading Lord Elgin's horses';[13]
- had overall charge of recovering cargo from Elgin's yacht that sank off a Greek island (see Chapter 14);[14]
- became the curator of The Elgin Museum in Park Lane where the marbles were first exhibited in London;[15]
- was proactive in negotiating the sale of the Elgin Marbles to the British Museum;[16] and
- was the only Foreign Office official called as a witness by the Select Committee in 1816. He lied to the Committee.

The Elgin Papers at the family archive at Broomhall, cited by Luciana Gallo, include seven volumes of correspondence. The first three are: Vol. I Lord Elgin to Lusieri 1799–1819; Vol. II Lord Elgin to Hamilton 1812–1836; and Vol. III Hamilton to Lord Elgin 1799– 1833.[17]

However, it is Elgin's letters to Hamilton prior to 1812, from 1799, that would shine a light on the role Elgin demanded of Hamilton in taking and transporting the Parthenon Sculptures.

Hamilton was made a trustee of the British Museum, a position he held for twenty years (1838–1858).[18] Hamilton can only have been proposed as a trustee by Elgin who, at the time, was himself a trustee (see Chapter 20).

---

[10] Gallo, *Lord Elgin and Ancient Greek Architecture*, p. 70.

[11] Checkland, *The Elgins, 1766–1917*, p. 46.

[12] Checkland, *The Elgins, 1766–1917*, p. 56.

[13] HMS *Diana*, Log Book, NA, ADM 51/1447.

[14] *Oxford Journal*, 5 March 1803, p. 4.

[15] Checkland, *The Elgins, 1766–1917*, p. 82, and on p. 67 a drawing by C. B. Cockerell, 1807.

[16] Checkland, *The Elgins, 1766–1917*, pp. 86–91.

[17] Gallo, *Lord Elgin and Ancient Greek Architecture*, p. 327.

[18] See Hamilton's *ODNB* entry.

CHAPTER 13

Should Elgin be paid the value of the marbles, or only his expenses?

It was maintained that if Elgin obtained the marbles only because he was Britain's ambassador, then the marbles automatically belonged to the public. And if the marbles belonged to the public, then Elgin could not sell them for their true value. He could, however, recover his expenses in obtaining them. But if Elgin obtained them as a private individual, then he could sell them for their true value.

The British Museum, under the heading 'The Legal Status of the British Museum's Collection', asserts that the Select Committee found that the collection had been legitimately acquired by Elgin as a private individual.[1] As already explained, the Select Committee did *not* find that Elgin acquired the collection as a private individual.

What, then, did Elgin get for the marbles and what were they worth? Establishing the value of the marbles when Elgin came to sell them is relevant because if he sold them for their true value, it confirms that he obtained them as a private individual and that the marbles were his to sell. However, if Elgin received nothing like their true value, then it suggests that the marbles were not his to sell.

Elgin did not sell the marbles for their true value. He asked £74,000 for the marbles. However, he requested this figure not because that was what the marbles were worth but because he claimed he spent £74,000 to obtain them.[2] Therefore, Elgin sought to fix a price that was equal to his expenses.

---

[1] 'The Parthenon Sculptures: Facts and Figures', Clause 3.1.

[2] Select Committee Report, p. 8.

However, Elgin sold the marbles to the British Museum for £35,000 (£24.3 million in current values), less than half his original asking price. In 1816, the public was led to believe that Elgin received £35,000 for the marbles; in reality he did not get anything like half of what he originally asked.

The Select Committee had been appointed to consider the marbles under four principal heads; one was the value of the marbles. The Select Committee did not call as witnesses any trustee of the British Museum or any curator at the museum. Therefore, the museum expressed no view as to the value of the marbles they were to acquire.

Elgin asked for £74,000 and the Select Committee obtained two valuations. One valuation was £25,000; the other was £60,800. The Select Committee then completely disregarded both valuations in deciding what to pay Elgin.

The valuation of £25,000 was based on the sum of £20,000, which the British Museum had recently paid for the Townley Marbles, a collection of Greek and Roman antiquities collected by Charles Townley on three visits to Italy. However, all expert witnesses questioned by the Select Committee on the merit of the Elgin Marbles as works of sculpture (including six witnesses from The Royal Academy) were unanimous that the marbles taken from the Parthenon were far superior to, and infinitely more valuable than, the Townley Marbles.

Even in 1815 it was acknowledged that the Townley Marbles could not compare with the marbles taken from the Parthenon. This was supported by the Italian sculptor Antonio Canova, described as neo-classicism's first great sculptor. Canova came to London in 1815, the year the Select Committee published its report, and after seeing the Elgin Marbles he allegedly said that if the British Museum paid £15,000 for the Phigaleian Marbles (another group of marbles acquired by the British Museum), then the Elgin Marbles were worth £100,000.[3]

In 2000, Mary Beard, Chair of Classics at Cambridge, wrote that the question of whether the Elgin Marbles were worth more or less than the Townley Marbles is hardly worth asking. She points out that the Townley Marbles are kept in a gloomy basement at the British Museum that gets few visitors and is

---

[3] Smith, 'Lord Elgin and his Collection', p. 333.

usually the first gallery to be closed when there are staff shortages.[4]

The second valuation of £60,800 obtained by the Select Committee was based on each piece of sculptured marble being valued individually. The list of pieces, with their values, was presented to the Select Committee, and includes as examples: Female group £4,000; Three horses' heads £2,000; Fifty-three pieces at £400 – and so on – totalling £60,800.[5]

No member of the Select Committee challenged or doubted the piece-by-piece valuation. Given that a collection is always worth significantly more than its individual constituent parts, Canova's valuation of £100,000 was not far wrong. Accordingly, Elgin's asking price of £74,000 was not unreasonable, even though it was based on his alleged expenses in obtaining them.

However, Elgin was initially offered only £30,000, a price that was wholly unrelated to the two valuations obtained by the Select Committee. In the 1816 Marbles Debate, it was stated that Elgin was offered £30,000, 'provided Lord Elgin *could make it appear* that his expense amounted to that sum' [emphasis added]. In other words, Elgin was clearly only going to get the expenses in obtaining the marbles and not their true value.[6]

Elgin, in his submission to the Select Committee, put his total expenditure 'prior to 1803 ... at £28,000. To which ... I have added fourteen years interest.'[7] Elgin added interest 'for 14 years at 5 per cent – £23,240'. However, as will be explained below, the £28,000 to obtain the marbles was entirely funded by the British government, and the government did not charge Elgin the interest he claimed. The fictitious interest was necessary to increase what Elgin maintained were his expenses to make up his asking price of £74,000. The Select Committee totally disregarded the interest claimed and set the original price at £30,000 because the real expenses of obtaining the marbles was established to be about £29,000.

---

[4] Mary Beard, *The Parthenon* (Cambridge, MA: Harvard University Press, 2002), p. 159.

[5] Select Committee Report, p. 29.

[6] Select Committee Report, p. 10.

[7] Select Committee Report, Appendix 6, p. 67.

In the Marbles Debate, it was stated that the original price offered to Elgin was £30,000 but that Elgin had an additional expense of £5,000. Therefore, it was judged that £35,000 was a reasonable price for the collection. While a price of £35,000 was suggested by the Select Committee, it was *not* a valuation of the marbles.

This was clearly not the true value of the marbles. This is confirmed by Smith, Keeper at the British Museum, who wrote that £30,000 had been suggested on various grounds but *not* as a valuation of the marbles, and that to the £30,000 a 'random £5,000' was added.[8] It is important to stress that a Keeper at the British Museum considered that the price was not based on a valuation of the marbles and that the addition of £5,000 was a completely random amount.

The Select Committee did not find that the value of the collection was £35,000 as the British Museum maintains. Elgin had to establish his expenses, and the fact that an additional expense of £5,000 increased the price, pound for pound, clearly establishes beyond any doubt that the price paid for the Elgin Marbles bore no relationship to their true value.

Today, the British Museum maintains that the Select Committee held the value of the collection to be £35,000.[9] This is another British Museum 'fact' that is wrong.

The price of £35,000 is way off all of the following: Elgin's original asking price of £74,000; the piece-by-piece valuation of £60,800; and Canova's £100,000 valuation. The significance of the price set as being equal to Elgin's expenses in obtaining the marbles is that it is an acknowledgement by the British government that the Elgin Marbles were procured by a British ambassador and that the marbles were not his private property to sell.

Elgin did not own the marbles on two counts. Firstly, bribes were paid; therefore, the marbles were not properly acquired. Secondly, even if the marbles had been properly acquired, they were not Elgin's to sell because he obtained them in his capacity as British ambassador.

---

[8] Smith, 'Lord Elgin and his Collection', p. 341.

[9] 'The Parthenon Sculptures: Facts and Figures', Clause 9.6.

But of much greater significance is the fact that if Elgin did not own the marbles, then he could not pass good title to the British Museum. The consequences of this, discussed in Chapter 28, are far reaching.

CHAPTER 14

Elgin, the Admiralty and a shipwreck

Elgin did not pay anything for the Parthenon Sculptures. Neither did he pay to have them transported to England. He did, however, have some expenses.

Elgin claimed an additional expense of £5,000 and this amount was added to the price paid to him. This chapter explains how and why a random £5,000 was added to the £30,000 originally offered to Elgin. The contention in this book is that the British government inflated the price by £5,000 as a reward for Elgin.

The Elgin Marbles were transported from Piraeus (Athens's port) to Malta and from Malta to England by the Admiralty in H. M. Ships. The Admiralty was responsible for the administration of the Royal Navy, and orders to the Admiralty came from the Foreign Office.[1]

The Admiralty transported everything for Elgin without any charge. In the House of Commons, Mr Gordon noted that the Elgin Marbles 'were brought over in ships of war and consequently at the public expense'.[2] The Admiralty was funded by the Treasury, so the government, not Elgin, paid these expenses.

It has been suggested by historians that Elgin made private arrangements with the captains of H. M. Ships and that the Admiralty was not in any way directly involved in transporting the marbles to England. Elgin stated in his submission to the Select Committee, 'I received much very friendly assistance from officers commanding King's ships, yet I employed two

[1] In 1964 the Admiralty became part of the Ministry of Defence.

[2] The Earl of Elgin's Petition, HC Deb, 23 February 1816, vol. 32, col. 823.

vessels of my own ... and several country ships.'[3] However, there is evidence that the Admiralty was very much involved in transporting the Elgin Marbles, and so too was the Foreign Office.

The Admiralty recorded every correspondence sent and received in annual digests and arranged it in over one hundred numbered headings with sub-headings, referred to as Cases. One of the Digest Cases was 'Freightage of Treasure' (Admiralty Digest Case 72.6). The 1810 Admiralty Digest records Hamilton's request, from the Foreign Office, that a ship be sent to Athens for Elgin's antiquities and a subsequent entry that Hamilton had been informed that the antiquities had arrived at Malta. Clearly both the Admiralty and the Foreign Office were very much involved.[4]

An entry in the 1812 Admiralty Digest ('Freightage of Treasure') is 'Letter from Rear Admiral Boyles stating his having sent out the [HMS] *Paulina* to Athens accompanied by the [HMS] *Pomone Transport* for the fragments of statues intended to be sent to England, and ordered Lord Elgin's Collection of antiquities to be put onboard the [HMS] *Orion Transport*'.[5] A letter in the Foreign Office register reads, 'Orders sent by the [name of ship indistinct] for the embarkation of Lord Elgin's antiquities.'[6] The Foreign Office was clearly involved.

It was widely reported in newspapers at the time that H. M. Ships were providing assistance to Elgin. For example, HMS *Prevoyante* was reported to be the 'store-ship for Lord Elgin'.[7] The same report stated that HMS *Braakel* 'has also brought home several cases for his Lordship [Elgin]'.

Checkland (the Elgins' biographer) wrote, 'In January 1804 the "first collection" of Marbles – fifty cases – weighing 150 tons – arrived in England by the *Prevoyante*.'[8] This sentence contains

---

[3] Select Committee Report, p. 65.

[4] Case 72.6, Admiralty Digest, 1810, NA, ADM 12/144.

[5] Case 72.6, Admiralty Digest, 1812, NA, ADM 12/156.

[6] Foreign Office Registers and Indexes of General Correspondence, Turkey 1810, 22 February, NA, FO 605/220.

[7] 'Sunday's Post', *Hampshire Chronicle*, 23 April 1804, p. 4.

[8] Checkland, *The Elgins, 1788–1917*, p. 62.

three factual errors. Firstly, the first collection of marbles arrived in 1802, not 1804 (see following paragraph). Secondly, in 1804 HMS *Prevoyante* did not transport marbles from Greece for Elgin but rather mummies from Egypt. The *Hampshire Chronicle* reported that 'several large chests within these last few days have been received from Egypt, containing various statutes and mummies sent to England by the *Prevoyante* store-ship for Lord Elgin'.[9] Thirdly, given the first two errors, the weight of the alleged fifty cases can only be imagined.

The marbles were transported from Greece as two collections, the first in 1802 (when Elgin was in Athens), the *Exeter Flying Post* reporting, 'This day [at Plymouth] fifteen cases of curious antique figures were landed from [HMS] *Diane* ... these curiosities were collected by Lord Elgin Ambassador at Constantinople chiefly in and about the ruins of Corinth and Athens.'[10]

The second collection arrived in England in 1812 when it was reported at Portsmouth, 'Fourscore [eighty] packages of Grecian mutilated Gods and Goddesses, some with heads, and many without are arrived and have been landed at Custom-house, consigned to Lord Elgin.'[11]

The captains of H. M. Ships made entries in log books stating that they transported cases specifically on behalf of Elgin. The original log books are at the National Archives. HMS *Prevoyante* Captain's Log records, on arrival in England, 'delivery cases of the Earl of Elgin'.[12] Other examples of entries in captains' logs include HMS *Mutine*: 'loading ... several cases belonging to Lord Elgin',[13] and HMS *Diane*: 'Getting Lord Elgin's stone out of the ship.'[14] Absolute reliance can be placed on the entries in H. M. Ships log books.

---

[9] 'Sunday's Post', *Hampshire Chronicle*, 23 April 1804, p. 4.

[10] 'Plymouth', *Exeter Flying Post*, 19 August 1802, p. 4.

[11] 'Ship News', *Morning Chronicle*, 11 July 1812, p. 3.

[12] HMS *Prevoyante*, Master's Logs, May 25, 1801 to April 10, 1804, NA, ADM 52/3665.

[13] HMS *Mutine*, Master's Logs, 10 December 1801 to 22 September 1802, NA, ADM 52/3232.

[14] HMS *Diane*, Captains' Logs including: *Albion*, *Daedalus*, *Diane*, *Diomede*, *Genereux*, 1797–1802, NA, ADM 51/1427.

In a letter Elgin sent when he was in Athens in 1802 he wrote, 'Lord Keith [an admiral] has been very obliging, by sending the [HMS] *Diana* frigate here: Capt. Stephenson has carried to Malta most of my acquisitions.'[15] In 1802, Lord Keith was onboard his flagship HMS *Foudroyant*, which was at Malta in February and at St. Helen's in July.[16] An admiral would not send a ship to Athens without directions from the Admiralty in London. The Admiralty's directions to HMS *Diane* are duly recorded in the Admiralty Index.[17]

Thus there is a seamless trail from Foreign Office directions (to send H. M. Ships), to Admiralty records, to entries in H. M. Ships log books and, finally, to the statement in the House of Commons confirming that the Elgin Marbles 'were brought over in ships of war and consequently at the public expense'.

However, while it is acknowledged by historians that H. M. Ships did transport marbles on behalf of Elgin there has been an attempt to remove, or to significantly downplay, the role played by the Admiralty. This is done by claiming, firstly, that ships other than H. M. Ships transported the bulk of the marbles and, secondly, that transportation from Greece to England was all done at Elgin's personal expense. These ships, according to Smith, Keeper at the British Museum, included *Dorinda, Costanza, Navigator, Mentor, Lady Shaw Stewart, Ann* and *Malabar.*[18] Historians have since placed reliance on Smith.

The *Dorinda* was a 320-ton Ragusan brigantine.[19] The *Costanza* was another ship from Ragusa, which in 1801 allegedly transported marbles destined for England from Piraeus to Alexandria in Egypt.[20] However, in his evidence to the Select Committee in 1816, Dr Philip Hunt, Elgin's chaplain and secretary, said, 'I had one [case] carefully packed and put on board a Ragusan ship, which was under my orders, from which it was transferred to a [HMS] frigate, and sent to England.'[21]

---

15 Smith, 'Lord Elgin and his Collection', p. 211.

16 *The Times*, 20 February 1802, p. 2; *The Times*, 6 July 1802, p. 2.

17 HMS *Diane*, Admiralty Digest, 1802, NA, ADM 12/94.

18 Smith, 'Lord Elgin and his Collection', pp. 256, 284, 209, 293 and 294.

19 Ragusa was a maritime republic on the Dalmatian coast.

20 Smith, 'Lord Elgin and his Collection', p. 209.

21 *Report from the Select Committee on the Earl of Elgin's Collection of Sculptured Marbles; &c.* p. 56.

Therefore, a Ragusan ship transported one case a short distance.

With regard to the *Navigator*, Checkland wrote, 'On 1 January 1812 came the great day when sixty-eight cases of Elgin's supplementary collection were landed at Malta in His Majesty's Ship *Navigator* bound for Deptford where it arrived on 25 May.'[22] This is impossible. In 1812 the Royal Navy did not have a ship named *Navigator*.[23] Checkland had access to the Elgin archives, but no blame lies with him: in 1916 Smith refers to HMS *Navigator* and the same voyage.[24] This means misinformation was planted in the Elgin archives over one hundred years ago – possibly two hundred years ago. If it is established that the Elgin archives contains one piece of misinformation, then it opens the door to there being more. When work on this book began, papers were searched when researchers left the National Archives in order to prevent theft. Now, all papers are searched before researchers *enter* a reading room because an historian was caught putting material *into* files at the Archives and then publishing more than one distorted history. It was not the first time misinformation had been planted in an archive and it will not be the last.

The *Lady Shaw Stewart*, as will be explained, was destroyed before the date she allegedly transported marbles. The *Mentor* is dealt with below.

Smith, who had access to Elgin's papers, claimed that Elgin's store-ship was not HMS *Prevoyante* but the *Scampavia*.[25] Despite extensive research, no trace of the existence of the *Scampavia* has been found, while the HMS *Prevoyante* Captain's Log records, on arrival in England, 'delivery cases of the Earl of Elgin'.[26]

The claims that Elgin's store-ship was not an H. M. Ship and the claims that other non-H. M. Ships transported the marbles from Greece to England at Elgin's expense are intended to

---

[22] Checkland, *The Elgins, 1788–1917*, p. 74.

[23] David Steel, *Steel's Original and Correct List of the Royal Navy* (London: Steel's Navigation Warehouse, 1812), pp.1–27.

[24] Smith, 'Lord Elgin and his Collection', p. 294.

[25] Smith, 'Lord Elgin and his Collection', p. 218.

[26] HMS *Prevoyante*, Master's Logs, May 25, 1801 to April 10, 1804, NA, ADM 52/3665.

remove the Admiralty – for which read 'the British government' – from being involved in obtaining the marbles.

The House of Commons Library produces independent and influential papers that are provided for MPs in support of their parliamentary duties. Members quote from the library papers during debates. The House of Commons Library paper 'The Parthenon Sculptures' gives an outline history of the long-running debate and whether or not the sculptures should be returned to Greece.[27] The paper covers transportation of the Elgin Marbles from Greece to England in two sentences.

The first sentence reads, 'Lord Elgin shipped the sculptures to his London home.' This inaccurate statement is what members of parliament rely on when the question of returning the Elgin Marbles to Greece comes before the House of Commons, as it frequently does. The second sentence in the paper concerning transportation relates to seventeen cases of sculptures sinking to the bottom of the sea. This claim is challenged below.

Downplaying the Admiralty's and the British government's role has succeeded brilliantly. For evidence as to how successful it has been look no further than what the Greek government says with regard to the transportation of the marbles on its official website: 'The shipping of these precious antiquities to Britain was fraught with difficulties, since they were moved from port to port. One ship sank and the sculptures, after prolonged exposure to the damp in various harbours, eventually arrived in England.'[28] Nothing is added to these two sentences, both of which are factually inaccurate. Therefore, at the time of writing, the Greek government is seemingly oblivious of the British government's role in the transportation of the marbles to England.

The Greek government's reference to a ship sinking leads to what may appear to be a digression, but it is not. The British

---

[27] Diana Douse and John Woodhouse, 'The Parthenon Sculptures', *www.parliament.uk.* 13 December 2012. <researchbriefings.files.parliament.uk/documents/SN02075/SN02075.pdf> Last accessed: 25 July 2916.

[28] 'The restitution of the Parthenon marbles: The review of the seizure', *Hellenic Ministry of Culture and Sports.* <odysseus.culture.gr/a/1/12/ea125.html>. Last accessed: 26 July 2016.

government offered Elgin £30,000 for the marbles *provided* he could make it appear that his expenses in obtaining them amounted to that sum. Elgin came up with an additional expense of £5,000, described by Smith as a random amount, and this increased the price to £35,000. The additional £5,000 that Elgin produced out of a hat was, allegedly, salvage costs.

It is claimed that a ship carrying some of the Elgin Marbles from Piraeus to England sank with her precious cargo. Depending on which sources you read, the ship sank in 1801, 1802, 1803 or 1804; depending on which sources you read, the ship that sank with the marbles was HMS *Mentor* or a merchant ship called *Mentor*. Uncertainties abound because according to Smith, who had access to Elgin's papers, no account of the voyage and shipwreck of the *Mentor* seems to have survived in those papers.[29] The reason why no records survive in his papers – or anywhere else – will become apparent.

In fact, the *Mentor* was not an H. M. Ship or a merchant ship; it was Elgin's private yacht. In Elgin's own words: 'The loss of my vessel (the *Mentor*) an English copper-bottomed yacht which was cast away off Cerigo with no other cargo on board than some of the sculptures.'[30]

Elgin claimed he bought the yacht 'solely' for the purpose of transporting his Greek antiquities from Piraeus to England.[31] However, the Admiralty was doing it for him free of charge. His assertion that he bought the yacht for this purpose is patent nonsense. HMS *Diane* arrived in Plymouth with Elgin's 'curiosities from Athens' in August 1802, a year before Elgin's private yacht sank in Greek waters.[32]

Elgin's yacht *Mentor* did sink off the Greek island Cerigo, also known as Kythera, 125 nautical miles from Piraeus. On board the small yacht were two crew members and a passenger; there was no loss of life. The contention in this book is that Elgin used the sinking of his yacht to fabricate a fictional salvage claim of

---

[29] Smith, 'Lord Elgin and his Collection', p. 240.

[30] Select Committee Report, p. 65.

[31] Turkey: Letters and Papers from the Earl of Elgin at Constantinople, to the Secretary of State: with Drafts to him. From January 13, 1803 to February 28, 1803, NA, FO 78/38, p. 29.

[32] 'Plymouth', *Exeter Flying Post*, 19 August 1802, p. 4.

£5,000 (£3.47 million in current values) for a three-year salvage operation to recover crates allegedly containing some of the Elgin Marbles. To add credence to the claim that *Mentor* was used to transport marbles it is alleged that the yacht had previously transported some of the marbles from Piraeus to Alexandria in Egypt.[33] The valuable marbles, destined for England, were unlikely to be sent via Egypt on a small yacht when H. M. Ships were freely available to Elgin and were actually landing marbles in England.

In his evidence to the Select Committee, Elgin did not mention the number of crates of marble that sank with his yacht. He did confirm that the cases which sank contained 'parts of the frieze and metopes'.[34] It is unclear who first claimed it was seventeen crates that were lost, but the number is now accepted as being authoritative.

In the Marbles Debate, Mr Bankes pointed out that seventeen crates represented nearly twenty per cent of the 'eighty cases' of marbles that arrived in England in 1814.[35] Today, the British Museum says there was a consignment of seventeen crates on Elgin's ship *Mentor* when she sank and every crate was salvaged at Elgin's expense.[36]

The loss of the *Mentor* gave rise to speculation that a part of the collection was irretrievably lost at sea, and this has been added to the British Museum's list of 'Further common misconceptions'.[37] The museum says nothing was lost at sea because Elgin salvaged all the crates. It is correct in stating that none of the crates were lost at sea, but for the wrong reason. None of the crates were lost at sea because it is a fiction that they ever went into the sea.

According to Elgin the marbles remained underwater for up to three years before they were salvaged. In a letter to the Select Committee, Elgin claims that 'the [salvage] operations … continued three years, in recovering the Marbles'. In a separate letter Elgin states that the salvage operation was 'not completed

---

[33] Smith, 'Lord Elgin and his Collection', p. 209.

[34] Select Committee Report, p. 66.

[35] Elgin Marbles, HC Deb, 7 June 1816, vol. 34, col. 1030.

[36] 'The Parthenon Sculptures: Facts and Figures', Clause 9.5.

[37] 'The Parthenon Sculptures: Facts and Figures', Clause 9.5.

till three years after the ship wreck'.[38] The yacht was a total loss and was not salvaged; the wreck continues to be visited by divers.

Given that it allegedly took three years to recover the crates of marbles from the Parthenon, there is a question that appears never to have been asked. Is there any evidence that any of the marbles suffered three years of saltwater damage? The British Museum does not comment on this in 'The Parthenon Sculptures: Facts and Figures'.

Marble is an extremely hard stone. It is not *highly* porous, but it is porous. A wine glass or coffee cup stain on a marble mantelpiece cannot be easily removed, if at all. It is established that salts from ground water, or from the air if near the sea, can damage sculptures, including marble. The Victoria and Albert Museum categorically advises to avoid using water to clean marble as it can cause damage.[39] Yet the world is to believe, and the British Museum seemingly accepts, Elgin's claim that seventeen crates (nearly twenty per cent of the Elgin Marbles received in England) were submerged in salt water for up to three years without being damaged.

It is simply not credible that the sculptured marbles, purportedly submerged in salt water for up to three years, are today indistinguishable from those that had not been in the sea. The fact that the marbles are indistinguishable means that marbles taken from the Parthenon never went into the sea and that Elgin created the fictional salvage expense of £5,000.

Smith, Keeper at the British Museum, wrote that the crates of marbles salvaged at Cerigo were transported from there by the *Lady Shaw Stewart* (an HMS Transport).[40] Smith gives the specific date this was done: 16 February 1805. However, the *Lady Shaw Stewart* cannot have transported marbles in 1805 because the ship was captured by the French off Lisbon in 1801 and destroyed.[41] *The Times* reported that the ship had been

---

[38] Select Committee Report, Appendix 5, p. 65.

[39] 'Conservation Case Studies: Cleaning Theseus and the Minotaur.' *Victoria and Albert Museum.* 25 July 2013. <www.vam.ac.uk/content/articles/c/cleaning-theseus-and-the-minotaur/>. Last accessed: 26 July 2016.

[40] Smith, 'Lord Elgin and his Collection', p. 260.

[41] 'Ship News Plymouth', *Hampshire Chronicle*, 9 March 1801, p. 4.

'taken and burnt by the French Squadron'.[42] Smith, who had access to Elgin's papers and found no account of the voyage and shipwreck of the *Mentor,* added that he could not find any record of how the salvaged crates had been transported to England after the *Lady Shaw Stewart* brought them from Cerigo to Malta. In the circumstances, this is hardly surprising because it is a myth that the cases ever went into the sea off Cerigo.

The British Museum's explanatory leaflet 'The Parthenon Sculptures' is intended to provide key information and present the main arguments of the debate as to whether the sculptures should be in Britain or Greece.[43] The museum's key information about how the sculptures were transported from Greece is that they were transported to Britain by Lord Elgin at his own expense. This information is factually incorrect.

---

[42] 'Captain Perry, of the *Lady Shaw Stewart*', *The Times,* 20 May 1806, p. 3.

[43] 'The Parthenon Sculptures.' *The British Museum.* <www.britishmuseum.org/about_us/news_and_press/statements/parthenon_sculptures.aspx>. Last accessed: 27 July 2016.

CHAPTER 15

Who bought the marbles from Elgin?

It is persistently and erroneously claimed by historians, writers and journalists that the British government bought the marbles from Elgin and presented them to the British Museum. This mistake is made because they rely on the British Museum's claim that the marbles were purchased by the British parliament from Elgin and presented by parliament to the British Museum. This claim is stated in bold letters in 'What are the "Elgin Marbles"?'[1] The British Museum's claim that parliament purchased the marbles and presented them to the museum is not correct.

In 2002, Tony Doubleday, the British Museum secretary, was quoted as saying that ownership of the Elgin Marbles was vested in the trustees of the British Museum by an Act of Parliament in 1816.[2] This, too, is incorrect.

As an example of the misunderstandings that have arisen from the British Museum's statements, take John Henry Merryman, Emeritus and Affiliated Professor in the Department of Art at Stanford Law School. He claims that the British government bought the marbles from Elgin. He then goes on to discuss the right of the Crown to the Elgin Marbles and the Crown's title to the marbles.[3] However, the Crown did not buy

---

[1] 'What are the "Elgin Marbles"?' *The British Museum.* <www.britishmuseum.org/explore/highlights/article_index/w/what_are_the_elgin_marbles.aspx>. Last accessed: 17 October 2014. No longer available.

[2] Julia Cahill, 'British Museum in legal fight over Elgin Marbles', *The Lawyer,* 11 February 2002. <www.thelawyer.com/issues/11-february-2002/british-museum-in-legal-fight-over-elgin-marbles/> Last accessed: 25 July 2016.

[3] John Henry Merryman, *Thinking about the Elgin Marbles: Critical Essays on Cultural Property, Art and Law,* 2nd edn (The Hague: Kluwer Law International, 2009), p. 36.

the marbles from Elgin; the Crown never had, nor professed to have, title to the marbles.

This is what happened: the British government made a grant to the trustees of the British Museum, which enabled the museum to buy the marbles directly from Elgin. The British Museum elsewhere corrects its online claim (that parliament presented the marbles to the museum) by confirming that the British Museum acquired the marbles directly from Elgin.[4]

The distinction as to who passed title to the marbles to the British Museum – the Crown or Elgin – is crucially important. This is because at the time of the sale there was a mortgage over the Elgin Marbles whereby the British government held them as security for a debt allegedly owed by Elgin to the Crown. Accordingly, the government, as a mortgagee in possession, could not acquire the marbles for £35,000, a price that was acknowledged at the time to be an undervalue. A mortgagee in possession (having seized the mortgaged property) cannot sell the property to itself at an undervalue. Therefore, Parliament agreed to grant £35,000 to the British Museum to acquire the marbles at a price that was not their true value.

The Act of Parliament in 1816 authorised the Lord High Treasurer of Great Britain to advance £35,000 to the British Museum trustees. The Act of Parliament further specifically instructed the trustees to pay the £35,000 to Elgin in exchange for his marbles.

However, this stipulation in an Act of Parliament was not adhered to. The trustees of the British Museum did not pay the £35,000 to Elgin. The trustees did not pay any part of the purchase price to Elgin. What took place in 1816 is most curious.

[4] 'The Parthenon Sculptures: Facts and Figures', Clause 9.6.

CHAPTER 16

The Elgin Marbles seized by the Crown

The Elgin Marbles have been debated for over two hundred years without mention of the mortgage, dated 4 December 1815, whereby the British government seized the marbles from Elgin.

During the Elgin Marbles Debate of 1816, Mr P. Moore 'desired to know whether they [the Elgin Marbles] were not in fact under sequestration at present by government for a debt due to the Crown by Lord Elgin'.[1] The answer is not recorded in Hansard, but the answer is: yes, they were. The government had indeed seized the marbles for a debt allegedly owed by Elgin.

The fact that Elgin mortgaged his marbles and that they were seized by the government has been completely overlooked in the two hundred-year debate. The revelation in parliament that the Crown had seized the marbles may be another reason, in addition to the mauling Elgin got during the debate, as to why the 1816 Parliamentary Debates are not available online. The reason why Elgin mortgaged the marbles has a significant bearing on the debate.

In 1815, the year before the Marbles Debate, Elgin entered into an indenture (a mortgage) over the Elgin Marbles. The indenture, dated 4 December 1815, was made between (1) Thomas Bruce, Earl of Elgin and Kincardine (2) Charles Rivington Broughton of Downing Street and (3) Frederick Booth and Horatio Leggatt, the Solicitors for the Affairs of Taxes.

---

[1] Elgin Marbles, HC Deb, 7 June 1816, vol. 34, col. 1040.

An original of the indenture is at the National Archives, but it is illegible.[2] However, in 1816 an abstract of the indenture was sent to the Attorney and Solicitor General; a copy of this is also at the National Archives. The abstract recites that Charles Rivington Broughton of Downing Street owed the Crown 'the sums of £98,000, £98,000, £100,000, £100,000 and £96,000' totalling £492,000.[3]

Broughton was a senior clerk at the Foreign Office, which in 1815 was in Downing Street.[4] Broughton, a mere clerk, allegedly owed the Crown £492,000. Elgin, an ambassador, allegedly owed Broughton £18,651.[5]

The Crown sought to recover a part of Broughton's debt, and on 15 September 1815 a writ was issued by the Receiver General of Taxes against Broughton seeking the recovery of '£54,000 and upwards'. The facts of the case are set out in the Treasury Solicitor's *Case Respecting Lord Elgin's Marbles: For the Opinion of the Attorney & Solicitor General*, dated 5 July 1816.[6]

The Crown did not seek to recover the full £492,000 owed by Broughton but a sufficient amount to cover what Elgin allegedly owed Broughton. Elgin's debt to Broughton was then seized by the Crown. Elgin could not pay and offered to place the Crown in a state of security by a lien (a charge or mortgage on property) on the marbles if proceedings to recover the debt could be suspended until parliament decided to buy the marbles from him. So the indenture was entered into between Elgin, Broughton, and Frederick Booth and Horatio Leggatt (Booth and Leggatt being the Solicitors for the Affairs of Taxes) who held the Elgin Marbles for the Crown.

The Member of Parliament who asked in the Marbles Debate 'whether they [the Elgin Marbles] were not in fact under

---

[2] Indenture between the Earl of Elgin and Charles Rivington Broughton appointing Frederick Booth and Horatio Leggatt trustees of the Elgin Marbles. A schedule of the Marbles is included, 1815, NA, EXT 8/8.

[3] Papers of the Treasury Solicitor and HM Procurator General, Re: Lord Elgin and the Elgin Marbles, British Museum, 1815–1817, NA, TS 11/981/3588.

[4] *The Royal Kalendar* (London: J. Debrett, 1800), p. 115.

[5] Papers of the Treasury Solicitor and HM Procurator General, Re: Lord Elgin and the Elgin Marbles, British Museum, 1815–1817, NA, TS 11/981/3588.

[6] Papers of the Treasury Solicitor and HM Procurator General, Re: Lord Elgin and the Elgin Marbles, British Museum, 1815–1817, NA, TS 11/981/3588.

sequestration at present by government for a debt due to the Crown by Lord Elgin' must have known they were. But how did a Foreign Office clerk come to owe the Crown £492,000 in 1815, which in current values is £341 million? Furthermore, how did Elgin, an ambassador, come to be personally indebted to a clerk at the Foreign Office?

One of Broughton's roles at the Foreign Office was to advance funds on an agency basis to Britain's ambassadors abroad. The advances were funded by the Treasury. This is evidenced by an advance of £2,000 made to Broughton in 1814, which he in turn made available to Sir Charles Stuart, Britain's ambassador in Paris. The advance became the subject of a dispute, and Broughton was a party to the legal proceedings.[7] The contention in this book is that the case in 1814 involving Britain's ambassador in Paris set a precedent for a fictitious claim in 1815 against Broughton and, in turn, against Elgin, Britain's ambassador in Constantinople.

Elgin, while ambassador, received amounts from public funds. This is confirmed in a number of sources, including the *Case Respecting Lord Elgin's Marbles: For the Opinion of the Attorney & Solicitor General.* The case recites, 'There was a considerable public account of Lord Elgin's as His Majesty's Ambassador to the Ottoman Porte [Turkey] during the years 1800–1 and 2 … It was probable that there would be a balance of about £29,000 due to the Public.'[8] These were the years that Elgin made commission and agency payments in Turkey, which he stated were 'very considerable'; that scaffolding was erected around the Parthenon in order to hack off marbles; and that Elgin 'employed three to four hundred people a day'. Therefore, Elgin's expenses would have been considerable. In his submissions to the Select Committee he claimed his expenses in obtaining the marbles were about £28,000 (which set the original offer price for the marbles at £30,000), which ties in with the balance of about £29,000 due to the public purse advance to him in Turkey.

---

[7] Charles Rivington Broughton: correspondence and accounts, 1808–1849, NA, C 103/5.

[8] Papers of the Treasury Solicitor and HM Procurator General, Re: Lord Elgin and the Elgin Marbles, British Museum, 1815–1817, NA, TS 11/981/3588.

However, although Elgin received significant amounts of public money while in Turkey, he did not receive any via Broughton. This is evidenced by Treasury files (T2 series) at the National Archives. The Treasury recorded all correspondence, including with the Secretary of State Foreign Department, and all payments made to Broughton. In 1801, the Treasury advanced £190 to Broughton (at the time a junior clerk) to pay Lord Carysford's bill for expenses in Berlin. In the same year the Treasury advanced amounts of £271, £78, £302 and £1,155 to Broughton, in each case recording the particulars. None of the payments to Broughton went to Elgin.[9]

The entries in the T2 series are chronological. Interspersed between the small payments to Broughton are large payments made directly to Elgin, that is, not via a clerk at the Foreign Office. For example, in 1801 Elgin received £25,000, £20,000, £20,000, £12,752, £10,729 and £6,085 from public funds, and fourteen other payments of between £5,000 and £1,000. The same pattern is repeated in the Treasury records for 1802. Meanwhile, Treasury records show that Broughton received two amounts of £162 and £137 (for expenses of named diplomats in Hamburg and Berlin respectively), while about £40,000 went directly to Elgin, ambassador in Constantinople.[10]

Some of the public funds paid to Elgin in Constantinople are easy to explain, but others are not. The ones that are easy to explain are those where the Treasury made payments for the army in Egypt. In 1801–1802, Britain fought a campaign against France in Egypt (when Britain took the Rosetta Stone from the French), and it was logistically more practical to supply the British Army from Turkey rather than from England. As ambassador, Elgin played a pivotal role, and the Treasury recorded, as an example, a letter from the Foreign Office stating that 'Lord Elgin has drawn £4,070 on account of the Commander General in Egypt'.[11]

However, the Treasury did not have a clue what some payments to Elgin were for. The Treasury Solicitors frequently

---

[9] Treasury: Registers of Papers, 1801, NA, T 2/36.

[10] Treasury: Registers of Papers, 1802, NA, T 2/38.

[11] Secretary of State Foreign Department, Treasury: Registers of Papers, 1801, NA, T 2/36.

wrote to the Foreign Office saying that Elgin had drawn bills on the Treasury, 'of which no advice has been received'. The payment of £12,757 in 1801 (mentioned above) is one such payment. There are others. Copies of the letters from the Treasury Solicitors are in a Foreign Office file at the National Archives.[12]

Elgin's correspondence with the Foreign Office, while he was in Constantinople, is in ten bound volumes at the National Archives.[13] The only correspondence between Elgin and Broughton is two extracts of letters. The first extract contains a list of Elgin's expenditure on public account.[14] The second contains a complaint by Elgin relating to the accounting of the disbursements of the embassy.[15] There has to be a reason why the Foreign Office file, which otherwise has complete letters, has only extracts of Elgin's letters to Broughton.

In his submissions to the Select Committee, Elgin stated that his expenditure in obtaining the marbles (up to 1803) was £28,000. The contention here is that Elgin used the £29,000 acknowledged to have been paid to him from the government to obtain the marbles. His expenses, as listed by him in his submission to the Select Committee, included commission and agency payments (bribes) in Turkey. Therefore, these were paid from public funds.

So Elgin received considerable sums of public funds while in Turkey, only some of which can be explained. But he did not receive any monies via Broughton because all payments to Broughton and how he used them are recorded by the Treasury.

---

[12] Turkey: Letters and Papers from the Earl of Elgin at Constantinople, to the Secretary of State: with Drafts to him. From January 10 1801 to May the 19 1801, NA, FO 78/31, pp. 113, 191, 266, 316 and 352.

[13] Turkey: Letters and Papers from the Earl of Elgin at Constantinople, to the Secretary of State: with Drafts to him. Commencing August 1799, NA, FO 78/24.

[14] Turkey: Letters and Papers from the Earl of Elgin at Constantinople, to the Secretary of State: with Drafts to him. From April 1, 1800 to July 22, 1800, NA, FO 78/29, p. 378.

[15] Turkey: Letters and Papers from the Earl of Elgin at Constantinople, to the Secretary of State: with Drafts to him. From March 1, 1802 to December 31, 1802, NA, FO 78/36, p. 119.

Broughton joined the Foreign Office as a junior clerk in 1789 and retired as a senior clerk in 1824. His thirty-five years uninterrupted service is recorded in the annual *Royal Kalendar* from 1789 to 1824, copies of which are at the National Archives. In 1815, a pretence was created that Broughton was in financial difficulties, and a writ was issued against him personally for some of the funds that he had received from the government and which he had advanced to ambassadors abroad. The pretence was created as a means for the government to seize the Elgin Marbles.

In 1815, Nicholas Vansittart, the Chancellor of the Exchequer, agreed 'to place the Crown in a state of security by a lien on the Marbles'.[16] As a result, the indenture (mortgage) was entered into on 4 December 1815, and it created a lien over the Elgin Marbles. For a lien to be effective there has to be physical possession, so the marbles were seized by the Crown. The money claimed from Elgin, as stated in the *Case Respecting Lord Elgin's Marbles: For the Opinion of the Attorney & Solicitor General*,[17] was advanced to him in Turkey 'during the years 1800–1 and 2', but the Crown made no efforts to reclaim the money until 1815. There is a reason why.

The indenture over the Elgin Marbles at the National Archives has been mutilated – torn to pieces. Forty-three fragments survive, some of which have been individually singed after being torn; these are affixed to eight sheets of parchment.[18] An expert at the National Archives could not explain how the document came to be in its present state, professing never to have seen anything like it. The explanation is simple. The indenture has been intentionally rendered illegible and only then put in the National Archives.

The fragments that survive are selectively chosen. The abstract mentioned above states that the indenture was made in

---

[16] Papers of the Treasury Solicitor and HM Procurator General, Re: Lord Elgin and the Elgin Marbles, British Museum, 1815–1817, NA, TS 11/981/3588.

[17] Papers of the Treasury Solicitor and HM Procurator General, Re: Lord Elgin and the Elgin Marbles, British Museum, 1815–1817, NA, TS 11/981/3588.

[18] Six sheets 67cm x 53 cm; the other two slightly smaller. Indenture between the Earl of Elgin and Charles Rivington Broughton appointing Frederick Booth and Horatio Leggatt trustees of the Elgin Marbles. A schedule of the Marbles is included, 1815, NA, EXT 8/8.

three originals, one for each party. The reconstructed indenture is made to appear to be an agreement between two individuals: Elgin and Broughton. The third party, Booth and Leggatt, the Solicitors for the Affairs of Taxes, has been removed. The surviving fragments include Elgin's and Broughton's seals and signatures, but not those of Booth and Leggatt, two government officials. The government's involvement has been expunged and then the illegible indenture made available to the public. The fragments contain descriptions of parts of the Parthenon Sculptures that are mortgaged.

The original of Elgin's indenture may be in the Elgin family archives at Broomhall. However, Sydney Checkland, the Elgins' biographer who had access to the Elgin archives, does not mention seeing it. But in one of his two sentences on the subject, he confirms, 'the Marbles were impounded by the Government'.[19]

The scheme in 1816 was to recover amounts advanced by the government to Elgin in Turkey from the sale proceeds of the marbles. In a letter dated 19 May 1816, Henry Charles Litchfield, Solicitor for the affairs of the Treasury, wrote that about £29,000 was due from Elgin to the public purse and that the amount would be withheld from the grant to be made to Elgin as payment for his marbles.[20]

In his written submission to the Select Committee, Elgin put his total expenditure in obtaining the marbles 'prior to 1803 … at £28,000' (after 1803 he added fictional salvage costs). Elgin's £28,000 stacks up with the Treasury claim that Elgin owed the public purse about £29,000. It also establishes that Elgin paid nothing out of his own pocket to obtain the marbles. The claim that obtaining the marbles bankrupted Elgin is a myth. Perpetuating the bankruptcy myth serves the case well for retaining the Elgin Marbles in the British Museum.

The writ issued against Broughton and the conversion of Elgin's public debt to a debt to Broughton were devices by which the Crown obtained possession of the marbles. The government had to take physical possession of the marbles as a

---

[19] Checkland, *The Elgins, 1788–1917*, p. 79.

[20] Papers of the Treasury Solicitor and HM Procurator General, Re: Lord Elgin and the Elgin Marbles, British Museum, 1815–1817, NA, TS 11/981/3588.

precautionary measure because there was a very real risk, given the widespread outrage against Elgin's act of taking the marbles and the anticipated mauling that Elgin would get in parliament in the Marbles Debate, that parliament would not approve the acquisition of the Elgin Marbles.

CHAPTER 17

Follow the money

Elgin did not receive the purchase price for the sculptures from the Parthenon that for over two hundred years have been called the Elgin Marbles. Who did?

In 1816, an Act of Parliament granted £35,000 to the British Museum and specifically directed the trustees of the museum to pay that amount to Elgin. This did not happen, even though the trustees were naturally anxious to act explicitly according to the Act.

Pickering & Smith, the British Museum's solicitors, wrote to all parties that the trustees of the British Museum wanted their payment for the Elgin Marbles to be unconnected with any private arrangement between others claiming interest in the Elgin Marbles, i.e. those having rights under the mortgage.[1] The solicitors' letter is an acknowledgement that the British Museum was fully aware of the existence of the mortgage over the marbles. However, Smith, Keeper at the British Museum, who had access to both Elgin's and the British Museum's papers and who wrote a forty-two page account of the 'purchase negotiations', does not mention the existence of the mortgage. Furthermore, Smith does not mention the British Museum's concerns that the specific direction in the Act of Parliament was not followed.

The direction in the Act to pay Elgin was overcome by Elgin waiving his entitlement to the £35,000 and agreeing that the British Museum should pay the whole amount not to him but as directed by the government – which was back to the

[1] Pickering & Smith to Trustees, 26 July 1816. Papers of the Treasury Solicitor and HM Procurator General, Re: Lord Elgin and the Elgin Marbles, British Museum, 1815–1817, NA, TS 11/981/3588.

government.[2] The money went back to the government because it was the government, not Elgin, who paid every pound to obtain the marbles.

The £35,000 advanced to the British Museum was recovered by the government in two separate amounts via different routes. In this way, the amount recovered was not seen to be equal to the price paid for the Elgin Marbles and the transaction revealed as the total sham it was.

First, the government paid £35,000 to the trustees of the British Museum; this was in accordance with the Act of Parliament. Secondly, the trustees paid £19,529 6s 10d (Elgin's alleged debt of £18,651 to Broughton, plus interest and expenses) to Booth and Leggatt, who were parties to the mortgage and who held the Elgin Marbles for the Crown. This money went straight back to the Crown.

The trustees then paid the balance of £15,470 13s 2d to Messrs Coutts & Co., Elgin's bank. However, the money did not go to Elgin's account. The amount was paid to a joint account in the names of Henry Charles Litchfield and Coutts Trotter.[3] Litchfield wrote that the amount due from Elgin while he was ambassador in Turkey 'would of course be withheld out of the Grant about to be made to Lord Elgin as the consideration money for the said Marbles'.[4] And so it was.

Litchfield and Trotter entered into a memorandum relating to the balance of £15,470 13s 2d paid to Coutts: that the amount should be held as security for loans made to Elgin while he was ambassador in Turkey.[5] This establishes that the amount advanced to Elgin in Turkey was greater than the amount he allegedly owed Broughton. However, in a letter of 21 October 1815 to William Hamilton, Under-Secretary of State at the

---

[2] Papers of the Treasury Solicitor and HM Procurator General, Re: Lord Elgin and the Elgin Marbles, British Museum, 1815–1817, NA, TS 11/981/3588.

[3] Papers of the Treasury Solicitor and HM Procurator General, Re: Lord Elgin and the Elgin Marbles, British Museum, 1815–1817, NA, TS 11/981/3588.

[4] Papers of the Treasury Solicitor and HM Procurator General, Re: Lord Elgin and the Elgin Marbles, British Museum, 1815–1817, NA, TS 11/981/3588.

[5] Memorandum dated 17 August 1816 signed by Henry Charles Litchfield and Coutts Trotter. Papers of the Treasury Solicitor and HM Procurator General, Re: Lord Elgin and the Elgin Marbles, British Museum, 1815–1817, NA, TS 11/981/3588

Foreign Office, Elgin claimed he owed Broughton £18,000, which the government seized.[6]

The entire amount of about £29,000, which it is claimed Elgin owed the government from his time in Turkey, could have been claimed in the writ against Broughton and the full amount recovered directly via Booth and Leggatt who held the marbles. However, this would not have looked good, because the price of the marbles was set at Elgin's expense of obtaining them, and it would have been obvious to everyone that the government had paid the entire cost of obtaining the marbles.

What was clever was the way the government used the funds advanced to Elgin 'during the years 1800–1 and 2'[7] to seize the marbles in 1815 as a precaution. If there had not been a real risk in 1816 that an outraged parliament may have refused to buy the marbles, then the amount advanced to Elgin to obtain the marbles would never have been demanded from him.

---

[6] The letter is reproduced in Smith, 'Lord Elgin and his Collection', p. 332.

[7] Papers of the Treasury Solicitor and HM Procurator General, Re: Lord Elgin and the Elgin Marbles, British Museum, 1815–1817, NA, TS 11/981/3588.

CHAPTER 18

An earlier mortgage on the marbles?

The mortgage on the Elgin Marbles is dated the 4 December 1815. However, a mortgage on marble sculptures taken by Elgin from the Parthenon may have been created by the government fourteen years earlier, in 1801, the year Elgin set out to get them.

In April 1800, Lord Grenville, the Foreign Secretary, wrote to Elgin in Constantinople acknowledging receipt of a letter from Elgin that the sender had marked 'private'. Elgin's letter enclosed a statement of disbursements and notice of drafts (cheques guaranteed by the issuing bank). Grenville complained to Elgin that the business in his letter had to be transacted in public and via official dispatches, not by private letter. Grenville rebuked Elgin because neither the account nor his private letter specified the amount of the intended drafts. He stressed to Elgin that expenditure without previous permission, except in cases of real necessity, was 'contrary to the Rules of the Foreign Service', and told him that no part of his business gave him so much trouble as the irregularity he constantly had to contend with on these points. He implored Elgin to adhere strictly to the Rules of the Foreign Service.[1]

Grenville was clearly a stickler for the rules. However, he soon waived the rules regarding payments to Elgin. This is evidenced by a letter headed 'Downing Street' (the Foreign Office) sent to the embassy in Constantinople on the 29 January 1801. The letter was sent on Grenville's directions and enclosed an indenture (a mortgage). The letter said that Grenville

[1] Turkey: Letters and Papers from the Earl of Elgin at Constantinople, to the Secretary of State: with Drafts to him. From April 1, 1800 to July 22, 1800, NA, FO 78/29, p. 111.

thought it would be advisable to omit in the signature copy of the mortgage all clauses relating to the payments to be made to Elgin.[2]

This letter raises a number of questions. What was Elgin mortgaging in 1801 and to whom? Why did Grenville not want the amounts paid to Elgin to be shown in the mortgage?

In his evidence to the Select Committee in 1816, Elgin said that before going to Constantinople he mentioned his proposal to Lord Grenville.[3] The contention in this book is that Elgin's proposal was not limited to making drawings and casts of the marbles, as he claimed before the Select Committee, but that it included taking sculptures from the Parthenon. It is further contended in this book that the British government funded the entire procurement operation of taking and transporting the marbles. If this is correct, then of course the government would have required security in 1801 over what was taken from the Parthenon. It is perfectly logical.

Files at the National Archives occasionally include redacted material. The redactions are clear for all to see. Some files include a notice, 'This file has been weeded.' The quaint alert is a euphemism for 'censored' and puts researchers on notice that correspondence and/or papers have been removed from the file. Elgin's correspondence with the Foreign Office, while he was in Constantinople, is in ten bound volumes at the National Archives.[4] Although there are no redactions and weeding notices, this correspondence has clearly been weeded. The letter sending the mortgage to Constantinople, discussed above, is the only letter in the ten volumes to mention the mortgage. The letter cannot stand alone; therefore the correspondence is clearly incomplete.

There is other missing material in the Foreign Office correspondence with Elgin. There is not a single letter in Foreign Office files relating to the transportation of the

---

[2] Turkey: Letters and Papers from the Earl of Elgin at Constantinople, to the Secretary of State: with Drafts to him. From January 10, 1801 to May 19, 1801, NA, FO 78/31.

[3] Select Committee, p. 17.

[4] Turkey: Letters and Papers from the Earl of Elgin at Constantinople, to the Secretary of State: with Drafts to him. Commencing August 1799 (NA FO 78/24).

marbles. Yet in other primary source documents there are records of Foreign Office directions to the Admiralty to send ships to transport Elgin's marbles. The Foreign Office must have received requests from Elgin, or on his behalf, when marbles were ready to be transported to England. How else could the Foreign Office direct the Admiralty?

A signed copy of the mortgage sent to Elgin in Constantinople in 1801 has not been found. However, the fact is that in 1801 there was a mortgage document, prepared by the Foreign Office and sent to Elgin in Turkey, in which Grenville specifically did not want the amounts paid to Elgin to be shown.

The *Case Respecting Lord Elgin's Marbles: For the Opinion of the Attorney & Solicitor General* [5] establishes that the 1815 mortgage over the Elgin Marbles secured amounts paid to Elgin while he was in Turkey – he was there from 6 November 1799 to 16 January 1803. There is no logical reason for the government to take a mortgage more than a decade after advances were made to Elgin. Therefore, the 1815 mortgage may have replaced the mortgage Grenville sent to Elgin in 1801.

The 1801 mortgage *had* to be replaced because a mortgage over the marbles created by Elgin in favour of the Crown for monies advanced to him in Turkey to obtain the marbles would have revealed Elgin to be the government's puppet. The 1815 mortgage interjected Broughton, a clerk at the Foreign Office. The amounts Grenville did not want shown in the 1801 mortgage would be the amounts paid to Elgin to obtain the sculptures from the Parthenon. The costs included employing four hundred workmen a day and paying the bribes in Turkey. Clearly, Grenville would not want those amounts shown.

---

[5] Papers of the Treasury Solicitor and HM Procurator General, Re: Lord Elgin and the Elgin Marbles, British Museum, 1815–1817, NA, TS 11/981/3588.

CHAPTER 19

How much did Elgin receive for the marbles?

It is difficult to establish precisely how much of the £35,000, granted to the British Museum to buy the Elgin Marbles, actually went into Elgin's pocket. It has been claimed that the remainder of the £35,000, after the government took £18,000, was paid to Elgin's other creditors.[1] However, if Elgin did have other creditors they did not get any part of the £35,000. This is because the government took the remainder via Litchfield and Trotter, just as Litchfield said would happen.

In 1971, the *New York Times* published a letter under the heading, 'The Present Lord Elgin Tots Up the Bill for Those Marbles'.[2] In the letter, the then Lord Elgin claimed his great-grandfather spent £85,000 of his own money to obtain the marbles and that he only received £12,500 of the £35,000 purchase price. The amount Elgin allegedly spent and the amount he allegedly received are addressed in turn.

Firstly, Elgin never claimed he spent £85,000. In his submissions to the Select Committee, he claimed his final cost was £74,000. However, this included £23,240 of interest.[3] The interest was a fiction which the government disregarded when Elgin's asking price of £74,000 was reduced to the initial £30,000. This represented the 'about £29,000' the government provided to Elgin in Turkey and which he used to obtain the marbles. The government did not charge Elgin interest. Elgin did not spend £85,000 of his own money. In fact, he did not spend any of his own money to obtain the marbles.

---

[1] St Clair, *Lord Elgin and the Marbles*, p. 261.

[2] Lord Elgin, 'The Present Lord Elgin Tots Up the Bill for Those Marbles' [Letter to the Editor], *New York Times*, 7 November 1971, p. 4.

[3] Select Committee Report, p. 8.

Furthermore, the letter to the *New York Times* claimed the salvage operations cost Elgin £10,000 when Elgin only claimed £5,000. In any event, the salvage costs were a fiction too.

Secondly, it is unlikely that Elgin received anything like as much as £12,500, as claimed. According to the letter in the *New York Times*, Elgin only received £12,500 because of the failure of the bank with which Elgin and the British government both had dealings. However, the balance of the £35,000 was paid to Coutts & Co., and the bank did not fail: it is doing well to this day.

The maximum Elgin may have received of the £35,000 is the £5,000 fictional salvage expenses. The government may have allowed Elgin to pocket this as his reward for obtaining the marbles. This reward (£3.47 million in current values) was Elgin's profit, and it establishes that the marbles did not bankrupt him.

If there had not been complicity and Elgin had not been allowed to get away with the fictional £5,000 salvage costs, then he would have received nothing at all for the marbles that bear his name. But then Elgin was Britain's ambassador and he did not pay anything for the marbles. The British Museum acknowledges this fact, stating that it is a popular misconception that Elgin purchased the Elgin Marbles.[4]

The reason why the government did not buy the marbles from Elgin and present them to the British Museum is because the government, having seized the marbles, would have bought them as mortgagee in possession. This has legal complications, one being that a mortgagee cannot sell mortgage property to itself at an undervalue. The price of £35,000 was a gross undervalue, as has been established by the fact that the piece-by-piece valuation of £60,800 was not questioned or doubted by the members of the Select Committee.

The grant of £35,000 was made to the trustees of the British Museum because the British government wanted to have clean hands. The government knew how the marbles were obtained, because the Treasury, via the Foreign Office, provided Elgin

---

[4] 'The Parthenon Sculptures.' *The British Museum*. <www.britishmuseum.org/about_us/news_and_press/statements/parthenon_sculptures.aspx>. Last accessed: 27 July 2016.

with the funds to obtain them. The Admiralty, as directed by the Foreign Office, transported them to England. This is why the government took direct action against the Elgin Marbles, seizing them as a precaution in case parliament was so outraged that it was unwilling to buy the marbles that Elgin had hacked from the Parthenon.

Chapter 20

The trustees – plus one

In 1815, the year before the Elgin Marbles Debate, Mr Rose asserted in the House of Commons that the trustees of the British Museum 'were determined to receive them'.[1] 'Determined' is a strong word. How far back did the determination of the trustees of the British Museum stretch?

The trustees of the British Museum who were determined to have the Elgin Marbles included: the Chancellor of the Exchequer (the Treasury provided Elgin with all the funds needed to obtain the marbles); the Foreign Secretary (the Foreign Office directed the Admiralty to make H. M. Ships available to transport the marbles to England); and the First Lord of the Admiralty (the Admiralty transported the Elgin Marbles to England free of charge).

It was Vansittart, the Chancellor of the Exchequer, who proposed to the House of Commons that the acquisition of the marbles should be referred to a Select Committee of the House of Commons.[2] Vansittart then appointed himself on the Select Committee.[3] The Select Committee did not ask Elgin about his time in Athens, even though Vansittart knew Elgin had been there. The Select Committee accepted William Hamilton's claim that the government had not provided Elgin with any assistance, even though Vansittart knew the government had provided all the funds to obtain the marbles and the Foreign Office directed the Admiralty to transport them to England.

---

[1] Petition of the Earl of Elgin respecting his Collection of Marbles, HC Deb, 15 June 1815, vol. 31, col. 830.

[2] Petition of the Earl of Elgin respecting his Collection of Marbles, HC Deb, 15 June 1815, vol. 31, col. 828.

[3] Smith, 'Lord Elgin and his Collection', p. 335.

Vansittart also knew that all witnesses questioned on the subject were unanimous that Elgin only got permission from the Turkish government because he was Britain's ambassador. He would have known that he only got the permission because he paid bribes in Turkey. Therefore, Vansittart would have anticipated the reaction of parliament when it came to debate the Elgin Marbles.

Even before Vansittart proposed the appointment of the Select Committee in 1815, he said in the House of Commons that he 'considered that the possession of these marbles would be a great acquisition for the public'.[4] Four months earlier, when he presented 'The Earl of Elgin's Petition' to the House of Commons, he had proposed that the Elgin Marbles should be acquired.[5]

The Select Committee was appointed to decide how Elgin got the marbles. Vansittart knew full well that Elgin got them with funds provided by the Treasury – Vansittart's own department.

Vansittart was also aware of the sentiments against Elgin's removal of the marbles, and he knew that Elgin would clearly face a storm in parliament. There was a real risk that parliament would throw out the proposal to acquire the Elgin Marbles. Vansittart was one of the trustees of the British Museum 'determined to receive them'. Therefore, it was him who agreed 'to place the Crown in a state of security by a lien (a mortgage) on the Marbles'.[6]

Elgin received advances from the Treasury while he was ambassador in Turkey. This is confirmed by the statement that 'there was a considerable public account of Lord Elgin as His Majesty's Ambassador to the Ottoman Porte [Turkey] during the years 1800–1 and 2'.[7] Elgin left Turkey in 1803, yet for the next twelve years the government did not seek to recover

[4] Petition of the Earl of Elgin respecting his Collection of Marbles, HC Deb, 15 June 1815, vol. 31, col. 828.

[5] Petition of the Earl of Elgin respecting his Collection of Marbles, HC Deb, 15 June 1815, vol. 31, col. 577.

[6] Papers of the Treasury Solicitor and HM Procurator General, Re: Lord Elgin and the Elgin Marbles, British Museum, 1815–1817, NA, TS 11/981/3588.

[7] Papers of the Treasury Solicitor and HM Procurator General, Re: Lord Elgin and the Elgin Marbles, British Museum, 1815–1817, NA, TS 11/981/3588.

advances made to him. In 1815, Vansittart sensed the tide was against Elgin when Newton told the House of Commons, 'He was afraid that the noble lord had ... committed the most flagrant acts of spoliation ... It was the duty of the House to ascertain the truth in these matters; for otherwise ... they would evidently sanction acts of public robbery.'[8] It was only after this that the amounts advanced to Elgin twelve years earlier were demanded and the marbles were seized.

Vansittart seized the marbles in December 1815. This was after the Select Committee had questioned all the witnesses but before its report was published and presented to parliament in March 1816. Vansittart had to seize the marbles before the publication of the report and before the Marbles Debate of June 1816.

After the Marbles Debate no time was wasted in getting the Elgin Marbles into the British Museum. The Act of Parliament that provided £35,000 to the British Museum was enacted in unusual haste. The entire legislative process was completed twenty-four days after the debate. The Act was approved in the House of Lords on 1 July 1816 without any debate, and received the Royal Assent on the same day.[9]

The 'random' £5,000 (so described by Smith, Keeper at the British Museum), added to the original price of £30,000, was a reward to Elgin for his role in obtaining the marbles. As an additional reward, the Act of Parliament that granted the £35,000 to the British Museum made Elgin a Trustee of the Museum. (The right to be a trustee of the British Museum extended beyond Elgin to every person who attained the rank of the Earl of Elgin.)

So Elgin was made a trustee of the British Museum by an Act of Parliament passed within a month of him being savaged in the Marbles Debate for being a plunderer. Elgin's appointment as a trustee was not in the motion debated in the House of Commons, nor was his appointment as a trustee mentioned

---

[8] Petition of the Earl of Elgin respecting his Collection of Marbles, HC Deb, 15 June 1815, vol. 31, col. 829.

[9] Second unopposed reading, 21 June 1816; third unopposed reading 25 June; passed 26 June; agreed by the House of Lords 1 July without debate; Royal Assent 1 July 1816.

during the course of the Marbles Debate. But his appointment is in Section 4 of the Act of Parliament.[10]

The British government knew that Elgin obtained the Elgin Marbles using funds provided by the government. The government also knew (because Elgin included it in his submission to the Select Committee of the House of Commons) that he paid commissions and agency (a euphemism for bribes) in Turkey. Elgin has been accused of cheating at marbles, but government ministers knew the score with him all along.

Given that the government funded the removal of the marbles and transported them to England, it raises the question: was Elgin, who made do with a small financial reward of £5,000 (small when compared to Canova's £100,000 valuation) and being made a trustee of the British Museum, no more than a front for the government? Would the British government fund the taking of another country's cultural property and put it in the British Museum? The answer is yes (see Chapter 27).

---

[10] *An Act to vest the Elgin Collection of ancient Marbles and Sculpture in the Trustees of the British Museum for the Use of the Public* (1816). 56 Geo. 3, c. 99, pp. 865–867, Section 4.

Chapter 21

Elgin, the government and the marbles

How involved was the British government in taking the Elgin Marbles? How much did the government know? To what extent did the government assist Elgin?

In his evidence to the Select Committee, Elgin stated that before he went to Turkey in 1799 he mentioned his proposal to make drawings and casts of the marbles to Lord Grenville, the Foreign Secretary, William Pitt, the prime minister, and Henry Dundas, the Secretary of State.[1] Clearly, Elgin discussed his proposal at the highest level of government. But a memorandum submitted to the Select Committee on Elgin's behalf states that the government did not interfere in Elgin's operations in Greece.[2] The memorandum further states that the government

> let it be distinctly understood, before his [Elgin] leaving England, that they could not authorize any expenditure, on an undertaking attended with so much uncertainty and risk; it being beyond doubt that, had they given instructions, or even any formal encouragement they would, with the advantages, have been liable for any loss.[3]

The government response to a proposal to make drawings and casts is overboard in the extreme. There can be no uncertainties, risks or losses attached to making drawings and casts. However, there would be if what Elgin was proposing was

---

[1] Select Committee Report, p. 17.

[2] Select Committee Report, Appendix 3, item 6, p. 62.

[3] Select Committee Report, Appendix 3, item 6, p. 62.

not merely making drawings but the wholesale removal of the most important part of another country's cultural heritage.

The memorandum asserts that the government was not prepared to authorise any expenditure. In order to satisfy the Select Committee that the government did not provide Elgin with any assistance, a letter was produced to the Select Committee which, it was claimed, would 'prove that ... Lord Elgin was carrying on his pursuits at his private risqué, and without any assistance whatever from Government'.[4] The letter is from Charles Townley, a collector of antiquities, including the Townley Marbles, to Mr Harrison, an architect employed by Elgin in Scotland. In the letter Townley merely acknowledges Harrison's comment that Elgin was not receiving any assistance from the government.

The letter does not prove what is claimed; in fact, the letter does not prove anything. No other evidence was submitted to the Select Committee to support the assertion that Elgin removed the marbles without 'any assistance whatsoever from Government'. The Select Committee did not call any Treasury officials as witnesses.

The Select Committee examined William Hamilton, the Under-Secretary of State at the Foreign Office. Hamilton admitted he was in Athens when sculptures were removed from the Parthenon, but he claimed he had nothing to do with them when he patently did. Hamilton was asked, 'Have you looked into Lord Elgin's correspondence at the Foreign Office, when he was ambassador, and do you find any correspondence on the subject of these Marbles?' Hamilton said he had, and he produced an extract of a letter from Elgin to Lord Hawkesbury (the Foreign Secretary) dated 13 January 1803.[5]

In the extract Elgin made two erroneous claims. The first was that he incurred 'many thousands of pounds ... in rescuing [Greek art] ... from ruin'. The second was that his lost yacht was 'solely employed' in transporting saved Greek art.[6] The extract Hamilton produced was dated three days before Elgin left Constantinople to return to England. Hamilton was asked, 'Is

---

[4] Select Committee Report, Appendix 7, p. 68.

[5] Select Committee Report, p. 25.

[6] Select Committee Report, p. 29.

that the only trace of reference to his Lordship's [Elgin's] pursuits in Greece, that you can find in the public correspondence?' Hamilton replied, 'I have not examined the whole of the correspondence, so that I cannot precisely say whether it is the only reference.'[7]

So Hamilton, the Under-Secretary of State at the Foreign Office, was allowed to get away with saying he had not read the whole of the Foreign Office correspondence with Elgin. There was clearly a cover-up in the evidence given to the Select Committee. There is documentary evidence that Hamilton knew more than he admitted and that Elgin *did* receive direct assistance from the government – funding and ships.

It has already been established that the Treasury provided Elgin with funds, evidenced by the Treasury T2 series files at the National Archives and by the statement, 'There was a considerable public account of Lord Elgin's as His Majesty's Ambassador to the Ottoman Porte [Turkey] during the years 1800–1 and 2.'[8]

The government also transported the Elgin Marbles at the public expense. Hamilton, at the Foreign Office, was actively involved in this. Given that the instructions to the Admiralty came from the Foreign Office, someone must have alerted the Foreign Office when an H. M. Ship was needed to transport the antiquities that Elgin took from Greece. However, Elgin's correspondence with Hamilton at the Admiralty and the documentary record of Elgin's correspondence with the Foreign Office concerning the sculptures from the Parthenon is not at the National Archives.

There is other correspondence missing. Elgin stood down as ambassador for five months to go to Athens. He cannot have done so without Foreign Office consent and approval, yet there is no correspondence relating to this. If Elgin wrote to the Foreign Office to say he wanted to go to Athens for a holiday or to study Greek art, then those letters would undoubtedly be among the letters and papers from the Earl of Elgin at Constantinople to the Secretary of State at the National

[7] Select Committee Report, p. 25.

[8] Papers of the Treasury Solicitor and HM Procurator General, Re: Lord Elgin and the Elgin Marbles, British Museum, 1815–1817, NA, TS 11/981/3588.

Archives. However, given there is absolutely no correspondence relating to Elgin standing down as ambassador, the presumption must be that he needed to go to Athens to oversee the four hundred workmen he employed there. This is correspondence that needed to be weeded.

In his evidence to the Select Committee, Elgin said that before he went to Turkey as ambassador he discussed his scheme with Lord Grenville, Mr Pitt and Henry Dundas. Soon after arriving in Constantinople Elgin wrote to Dundas, but what he wrote remains secret, as Elgin intended. After his opening paragraph Elgin switched to a cypher: '... 3403. 4030. 1632 ...' Elgin's letter has one hundred and eighty-three sets of numbers, each representing a word or phrase. The cypher Elgin employed was for specific use with Dundas, because Elgin adds a postscript, in English, that he has not yet got a cypher with Lord Mornington.[9]

The scheme and operation to take marbles from the Parthenon, the Temple of Athena Nike, the Propylaea, the Erechtheion, the Theatre of Bacchus, and from other sites in Greece (all of which Elgin did) was beyond any one man. It was a massive undertaking. Elgin employed three to four hundred people a day. The operation was only possible because the Treasury, the Foreign Office and the Admiralty were all involved. Elgin, as Britain's ambassador in Constantinople, was a cog, conveniently placed to bribe the Turkish authorities in Turkey.

---

[9] Letter of 17 November 1799, Turkey: Letters and Papers from the Earl of Elgin at Constantinople, to the Secretary of State: with Drafts to him. From August 14, 1799 to December 31, 1799, NA, FO 78/24.

CHAPTER 22

A lack of candour

The parliamentary debates, spanning over two hundred years, are available online on the Historic Hansard website. However, records of two years are missing; one missing year is 1816. This may be an attempt to conceal the mauling that Elgin received in the House of Commons in the Elgin Marbles Debate of 7 June 1816. It may also be an attempt to conceal the fact, raised during the debate, that the Crown had seized the Elgin Marbles.

The absence of the debate online makes it difficult for Elgin to be judged by the standards of his day, as the British Museum maintains he must.[1]

* * *

The absence of the 1816 Marbles Debate online is not the only matter of serious concern.

The amount Elgin paid in commission and agency fees in Turkey in connection with taking the Elgin Marbles was deleted in the Select Committee Report.[2] In his subsequent submission, the entire line relating to the payments has been deleted.

The role played by the government and the Admiralty has been significantly downplayed by claims made to the Select Committee that Elgin received no assistance from the government, and by claims that ships other than H. M. Ships transported the Elgin Marbles. Furthermore, there are claims that transportation of the marbles was all at Elgin's personal expense.

---

[1] 'The Parthenon Sculptures: Facts and Figures', Clause 10.2.

[2] Select Committee Report, Appendix 5, p. 65.

The correspondence between the Foreign Office and Elgin has been weeded without putting researchers on notice. All correspondence relating to transport arrangements has been removed, as has all but one letter relating to the mortgage sent by the Foreign Office to Elgin in Turkey in 1801.

The indenture (mortgage) over the Elgin Marbles dated 4 December 1815 was signed in three originals. The original copy at the National Archives has been deliberately torn to pieces and then partly reconstituted.[3]

Smith, who devotes forty-two pages of his long essay 'Lord Elgin and his Collection' to the British Museum's 'Purchase Negotiations' with Elgin, does not mention the mortgage over the Elgin Marbles. Furthermore, he does not mention the British Museum's concerns that the £35,000 was not paid to Elgin as specifically directed in the Act of Parliament.

In a Treasury memorandum on the British Museum Bill 1963, a section dealing with the Elgin Marbles was removed before the Treasury file was put in the National Archives (see Chapter 24).

The British Museum's case to retain the Elgin Marbles is built on half-truths and untruths which include the following:

- that the Select Committee of the House of Commons was of the opinion that Elgin had acted with permission as a private individual. [4]
- that Elgin gave presents to authorities in Athens that did not amount to £600,[5] but paid nothing to authorities in Turkey to obtain the marbles. In his expenses, Elgin states that he paid considerable amounts in Turkey.
- that Elgin transported the marbles to Britain at his own expense.[6] Mr Gordon categorically stated in the House of Commons that the Elgin Marbles were brought to England in H. M. Ships and at the public expense.[7]

---

[3] Indenture between the Earl of Elgin and Charles Rivington Broughton appointing Frederick Booth and Horatio Leggatt trustees of the Elgin Marbles. A schedule of the Marbles is included, 1815, NA, EXT 8/8.

[4] 'The Parthenon Sculptures: Facts and Figures', Clause 9.2.4.

[5] 'The Parthenon Sculptures: Facts and Figures', Clause 9.3.

[6] 'The Parthenon Sculptures.' *The British Museum.* <www.britishmuseum.org/about_us/news_and_press/statements/parthenon_sculptures.aspx>.

[7] The Earl of Elgin's Petition, HC Deb, 23 February 1816, vol. 32, col. 823.

- that the Select Committee held that the value of Elgin's collection was £35,000 when this was clearly related to the expenses incurred to obtain them.[8] Elgin's additional alleged expense of £5,000 increased the price by £5,000.
- that the 'Elgin Collection' included other materials besides objects in stone, such as jewellery (no jewellery is mentioned in the Select Committee Report), but omitted any mention of the 880 Greek coins in the Elgin Collection.[9]
- that the Act of Parliament which granted £35,000 to the British Museum was a Local and Personal Act.[10] The Act is a Public Act and will not be found by searching through endless Local and Personal Acts.
- that parliament acquired the Elgin Marbles from Elgin and presented them to the British Museum.[11] Parliament did not acquire the marbles from Elgin; it gave the British Museum the money to buy them.
- that Elgin was a man of the Enlightenment and what he did was deemed to be acceptable in his day.[12] Elgin was savaged in the House of Commons' Elgin Marbles Debate, which establishes that what he did was far from acceptable in his day.

---

[8] Select Committee Report, p. 10.

[9] 'The Parthenon Sculptures: Facts and Figures', Clause 1.2.

[10] 'The Parthenon Sculptures.' *The British Museum.* <www.britishmuseum.org/about_us/news_and_press/statements/parthenon_sculptures.aspx>.

[11] 'What are the "Elgin Marbles"?' *The British Museum.* Last accessed: 17 October 2014. No longer available.

[12] 'The Parthenon Sculptures: Facts and Figures', Clause 10.2.

Chapter 23

A symbolic gesture

In 2006, the University of Heidelberg returned a fragment of the Parthenon Marbles to Greece. The fragment was registered as being in the university's collection in 1871. It is believed that the fragment was taken from the Parthenon by a traveller to Greece some seventy years after Elgin.

In a statement, the University of Heidelberg said that the decision to return the fragment to Greece was 'guided by the scholarly aim of promoting the unification of the Parthenon as a unique monument of world culture'.[1] At the presentation of the fragment, the Greek Minister of Culture said, 'In essence, the university made the first step in the promotion of the restitution of the Parthenon Marbles, realizing that there cannot be any scientific, or legal or moral argument for their retaining.'[2]

Surprisingly, the eleventh Lord Elgin admitted in 1983 that he was not in principle opposed to the Elgin Marbles being returned to Greece.[3] He said he would be in favour of their return provided there was a great museum in Athens to house them and that *all* the marbles taken from the Parthenon were returned, not just the ones in the British Museum. The new

---

[1] 'Heidelberg frieze fragment return & its implications for the Elgin Marbles', *Elginism.* 12 September 2006. <www.elginism.com/elgin-marbles/heidelberg-frieze-fragment-implications-for-the-elgin-marbles/20060912/535/>. Last accessed: 26 July 2016.

[2] 'Speech of the Minister of Culture Mr Georgios Voulgarakis at the Presentation of the First Fragment of the Parthenon Marbles that was returned in Greece by the University of Heidelberg', *Hellenic Ministry of Culture and Sports,* 5 September 2006. <odysseus.culture.gr/a/1/12/files/omilia_05_09_06_en.pdf>. Last accessed: 26 July 2016.

[3] Hugo Davenport, 'Elgin Marbles surprise', *The Observer,* 15 May 1983, p. 4.

Acropolis Museum has since been built specifically to house the Parthenon Sculptures.

The marbles from the Parthenon that are not in Athens today are reportedly held in the following places:

- the University of Würzburg (one marble)
- the National Museum, Copenhagen (two marbles)
- the Glyptothek, Munich (two marbles)
- the Kunsthistorisches Museum, Vienna (three marbles)
- the Vatican Museum (three or four marbles)
- the Louvre (six or seven marbles)
- the British Museum (eighty-two marbles from Elgin)
- the British Museum (unknown number of marbles from sources cited below).

The eighty-two marbles in the British Museum acquired from Elgin are listed and described in an appendix to the Select Committee Report.[4] In addition, there are an undisclosed number of marbles from the Parthenon in the British Museum. The museum says these have no connection with Elgin.[5] According to a British Museum publication these were received from the following eight sources: The Society of Dilettanti; The Royal Academy (previously owned by the Society of Dilettanti); J. J. Dubois; J. Smith Barry; C. R. Cockerell; the Duke of Devonshire; the Pourtalès Collection; and J. J. Dumville Botterell.[6]

Yet the British Museum has still more marbles from the Parthenon that it acquired from other sources. In 1866, the museum acquired a youthful male head from the frieze of the Parthenon, formerly 'in the possession of Mr. Fauvel of Athens'.[7] In 1881, the museum acquired two fragments from the northern and eastern friezes of the Parthenon, 'formerly in the possession of Mr. Steinhäuser, in Karlsruhe'.[8]

---

[4] Select Committee Report, Appendix 11, pp. 70–7.

[5] 'The Parthenon Sculptures: Facts and Figures', Clause 1.3.

[6] B. F. Cook, *The Elgin Marbles* (London: British Museum Press, 1997), pp. 89–90.

[7] British Museum: Accounts ... for the year ending 31 March 1881, HC Parliamentary Papers, Accounts and Papers, 262, 1881, p. 16.

[8] British Museum: Accounts ... for the year ending 31 March 1881, HC Parliamentary Papers, Accounts and Papers, 262, 1881, p. 19.

The British Museum may have as many as a hundred or more pieces of marble from the Parthenon.

The museum maintains that all of the marbles from the Parthenon in its possession are on permanent display.[9] However, there are only *ninety* marbles from the Parthenon on display in the Duveen Gallery at the British Museum.

One of the arguments constantly advanced for keeping the Parthenon Sculptures in the British Museum is that more people would see them there than if the marbles were in Athens. Yet some of the sculptures may be kept in storage in the British Museum.

---

[9] 'The Parthenon Sculptures: Facts and Figures', Clause 1.4.

CHAPTER 24

The British Museum Act 1963: an artificial barrier

In 1961, the Foreign Office proposed that the Elgin Marbles should be returned to Greece. The British Museum was adamantly against such a proposal.

The Foreign Office's wishes and the British Museum's curt rejection even to discuss the matter are recorded in the Treasury file at the National Archives, 'British Museum: Return of the Caryatid and the Elgin Marbles to the Greek Government, 1961–1966'.[1] (Elgin also took the Caryatid Marbles from the Erechtheion on the Acropolis.)

The Treasury, as the source of finance for the British Museum, is responsible for answering parliamentary questions relating to the museum, which is why the Treasury maintains files relating to the British Museum.

In 1961, Mr Noel-Baker asked Prime Minister Harold Macmillan in the House of Commons, 'would the Prime Minister not consider returning the Elgin Marbles, on the grounds of generosity, to a very loyal ally?'.[2] In his reply, Macmillan was careful not to exclude the possibility of returning the marbles to Greece. He said he would consider it.

There was consternation at the British Museum. On the day Macmillan gave his reply in parliament, Mr Bridgewater, the Director of the British Museum, telephoned the Treasury to express his apprehension at the possible implications of Macmillan's answer.[3]

---

[1] British Museum: Return of the Caryatid and the Elgin Marbles to the Greek Government, 1961–1966, NA, T 227/2252.

[2] Elgin Marbles, HL Deb, 9 May 1961, vol. 640, col. 221.

[3] British Museum: Return of the Caryatid and the Elgin Marbles to the Greek Government, 1961–1966, NA, T 227/2252.

After Macmillan's encouraging reply, the Foreign Office continued to press for the return of the marbles to Greece. This prompted a memo from one Treasury official to another suggesting that the Treasury was going to be squeezed most uncomfortably between the Foreign Office and the British Museum.[4]

It was against this backdrop of pressure from the Foreign Office to return the Elgin Marbles that the British Museum Act 1963 was enacted.

The Treasury prepared a memorandum on the British Museum Bill with the heading 'Major Notes' and 'Minor Notes'. The first of the fifteen Major Notes is: 'Reasons for introducing the Bill'; the eighth Major Note is: 'The Elgin Marbles'.[5] This shows that the Elgin Marbles were a major issue when the British Museum Bill was being considered. However, whatever the Treasury wrote on the British Museum's behalf regarding the Elgin Marbles in relation to the British Museum Bill is not known, because that section of the memorandum was removed before the Treasury file was put in the National Archives.

Nevertheless, it is known that the British Museum trustees wanted the British Museum Act to create a barrier that would prevent trustees from returning objects in the collections. This is known because another Treasury memorandum on the British Museum Bill states, 'The Trustees see strong objections of principle to any provision enabling them to transfer objects from their collections, even within a strictly limited field.'[6]

The trustees' strong objections led directly to the enactment of Section 3(4) (under 'Keeping and inspection of collections') and 5 ('Disposal of objects') of the British Museum Act 1963. These sections prohibit the trustees from disposing of objects unless the objects are duplicates; or were made after 1850 and are of printed matter and the museum has a copy; or if the objects are unfit to be kept in the collections.

So when Lord Jenkins of Putney called for the government to return the Elgin Marbles to Greece in 1982, the government

---

[4] British Museum: Return of the Caryatid and the Elgin Marbles to the Greek Government, 1961–1966, NA, T 227/2252.

[5] Background papers to British Museum Act 1963, 1962–63, NA, T 218/548.

[6] Background papers to British Museum Act 1963, 1963, NA, T 218/549.

relied on the British Museum Act 1963. Lord Jenkins asked whether the government would return the Elgin Marbles to Greece. The Earl of Avon replied on behalf of the government: 'My Lords, no, it is not the Government's intention to do so. The ownership of the Elgin Marbles is vested in the trustees of the British Museum under an Act of Parliament and my honourable friend the Minister for the Arts sees no cause for amending legislation.'[7]

In turn, the British Museum also relies on the British Museum Act 1963 in its case to retain the marbles, stating that the trustees are not permitted to return the marbles to Greece.[8]

However, the 1963 Act is an artificial barrier. The provision in the Act that prevents the transfer of objects from the collection can be removed by parliament. It is easily done. It may be believed that the British Museum Act 1963 will protect the Elgin Marbles in perpetuity, but a willing parliament could remove the marbles from the British Museum and send them back to Greece at a stroke.

The British Museum Act 1963 repealed the 1816 Act that granted £35,000 to the British Museum. The repeal removed the right of every person who attained the rank of the Earl of Elgin to be a trustee of the British Museum.[9] Much to the grief of the Elgin family, and to protestations in parliament, the Elgin family statutory right was removed by parliament in an instant, as were the rights of five other families to be trustees of the British Museum. Parliament could just as easily repeal the 1963 Act, or at least the sections that constitute an artificial barrier.

In 2015, the British Museum rejected UNESCO's offer to mediate in the long-running dispute over the Elgin Marbles (see Chapter 28). In a letter to UNESCO, the British Museum pointed out that it is not a government body and that its collections do not belong to the British government. This is correct, but parliament can, and did in 1963, change the composition of the Board of Trustees of the British Museum. However, it is unlikely that the trustees would refuse to return the Elgin Marbles if parliament legislated that they should be

---

[7] The Elgin Marbles, HL Deb, 15 February 1982, vol. 427, col. 361–3.

[8] 'The Parthenon Sculptures: Facts and Figures', Clause 3.2.

[9] British Museum Act 1963, Fourth Schedule.

returned to the Greek government. If they did, parliament would once again change the composition of the trustees.

The British Museum's letter to UNESCO also described the Elgin Marbles and the museum's collections as being inalienable – meaning they are incapable of being surrendered or transferred. This is only true until such time as parliament decides that objects in the British Museum collections must be surrendered. There are two precedents.

In 1980, the Tasmanian Aboriginal Centre requested that the remains of seventeen Tasmanian Aboriginals be returned to Tasmania. The remains, taken around 1850, were kept in the British Museum until natural history collections were transferred (by an Act of Parliament) to the Natural History Museum. The remains were not returned as requested, and the dispute dragged on for twenty years, ending up in the High Court in London. The High Court judge suggested mediation. The matter was resolved when, in 2004, parliament changed the law to permit human remains in museums in the United Kingdom to be surrendered. The Human Tissue Act 2004, Section 47, grants 'power to de-accession human remains ... This section applies to ... the Trustees of the British Museum'.[10] In 2005, after a twenty-five year dispute, the remains were finally returned to Tasmania where they rightfully belong.

The second time the law was changed to allow the British Museum to surrender objects is the Holocaust (Return of Cultural Objects) Act 2009. The law which permits the return of objects looted during the Second World War applies to the trustees of the British Museum.

While there is a statutory prohibition on the British Museum disposing of objects, the Human Tissue Act 2004 and the Holocaust (Return of Cultural Objects) Act 2009 clearly establish that the Elgin Marbles will remain in the British Museum until such time as parliament decides they should be returned to the Greek government.

---

[10] Human Tissue Act 2004, Section 47 (1).

CHAPTER 25

Parliament, the public and the Elgin Marbles

Members of parliament have called on the British government to return the Elgin Marbles to Greece in: 1941, 1942, 1950, 1954, 1958, 1959, 1961, 1962, 1965, 1982, 1983, 1984, 1985, 1987, 1988, 1990, 1992, 1994, 1996, 1997, 1998, 2000, 2001, 2002, 2003, 2004, 2007, 2012, 2015 and, most recently, in 2016, the bicentenary of their acquisition by the British Museum.

The requests to return the Elgin Marbles can be read online. The requests are made in debates in the House of Lords and in the House of Commons, in Early Day Motions, twelve since 1995 (formal motions submitted for debate in the House of Commons), in questions in the House of Commons, and in a Private Members Bill.[1]

'The Parthenon Sculptures (Return to Greece) Bill 2016–2017' is before parliament at the time of writing.[2] The bill, supported by a cross-party group of members of parliament, seeks to amend the British Museum Act 1963 and return the Parthenon Sculptures to the Greek government.

Extraordinarily, the members of parliament who for seven decades have called for the restoration of the marbles to Greece did so without knowing the full facts of the case or how the marbles had been taken. The same applies to members of the public in favour of returning the marbles and to politicians and academics worldwide who have called for the marbles to be returned. None has any idea of the mortgage on the Elgin Marbles, how it came to be created or the extent of the British

---

[1] See *Hansard Online* <https://hansard.parliament.uk/> and House of Lords Hansard archives <www.parliament.uk/business/publications/hansard/lords/>. Use the search term: Elgin Marbles.

[2] First reading: House of Commons 11 July 2016; second reading: 20 January 2017.

government's involvement in taking the marbles from the Parthenon.

While in 1961 Macmillan was undecided about the marbles, some prime ministers have been in favour of returning them (Wilson and Callaghan) and some have been against (Thatcher, Blair and Cameron). Theresa May has yet to say.

In 1998, a poll carried out by Ipsos MORI asked, 'If there were a referendum on whether or not the Elgin Marbles should return to Greece, how would you vote?' Thirty-nine per cent said they would return them to Greece, fifteen per cent were in favour of keeping them in the British Museum and eighteen per cent would not vote. In 2002, Ipsos MORI put the same question: forty per cent were in favour of returning them to Greece and only sixteen per cent in favour of keeping them in the British Museum.

In 2012, the Museums Association conducted a poll asking, 'Should the Parthenon Sculptures be returned?' Seventy-three per cent said yes; twenty-seven per cent said no.[3]

In 2014, a YouGov poll for *The Times* found that forty-nine per cent of the public said the Elgin Marbles should be returned to Greece while twenty-six per cent said they should remain in the British Museum, a two-to-one margin in favour of the marbles being returned to Greece.[4]

The calls for the return of the Elgin Marbles to Greece are persistent and will continue. This is because the sculptures taken from the Parthenon are unquestionably the world's most important unresolved cultural property issue. The issue will not go away – not in Greece, not in parliament, not worldwide – until it is resolved. This is a snapshot of the worldwide attention the Elgin Marbles received in a single year (2000):

- Turkey expressed support for the return of the Elgin Marbles to Greece. Turkey's Foreign Minister, Ismail Cem, said, 'I fully support the Greek government's effort and quest to have their properties back.'[5]

---

[3] 'Should the Parthenon Sculptures be returned?' *Museums Association.* <www.museumsassociation.org/museums-journal/news/01062012-should-parthenon-marbles-be-returned-to-greece>. Last accessed: 27 July 2016.

[4] Sam Coates, 'Public split by museum's decision to lend Marbles', *The Times*, 14 December 2014, p. 7.

[5] 'Turkey backs Greek fight to regain Elgin Marbles', *Reuters News*, 5 February 2000.

- United States President Bill Clinton said that if it were up to him, he would return the marbles.[6]
- Chinese President Jiang Zemin called for Britain to return the Elgin Marbles to Greece.[7]
- Former Australian prime ministers Gough Whitlam and Malcolm Fraser and other politicians joined a campaign to return to Parthenon Marbles to Greece.[8]
- Britain boycotted a United Nations convention on cultural artefacts, because if Britain signed the United Nations Unidroit Convention it risked forcing Britain to return the Elgin Marbles.[9]
- Greece's ambassador to Britain boycotted a royal dinner at the British Museum when he learned that the dinner was to be served in the Duveen Gallery, which housed the Parthenon Sculptures.[10]

The Greek ambassador's boycott drew attention to the fact that corporate clients and wealthy individuals were being permitted by the British Museum to party in the gallery with the Elgin Marbles. Guests and waiters would sometimes dress in Greek costume, and decorations could be put up provided they were tasteful and not draped over the marbles. The fee to hire the marbles for a night (excluding food, drink and staff) was £35,000. This is the amount parliament granted the British Museum in 1816 to acquire the marbles.

The disclosure that the British Museum was using the Elgin Marbles for themed dinners shocked academics, members of parliament and even former trustees of the British Museum. A professor of classical archaeology at Cambridge University said he was 'speechless – gobsmacked frankly'. A Member of Parliament was dismayed at the attitude of the British Museum. A former trustee of the National Museum of Scotland described

---

[6] 'US First Lady asks Britain to return Elgin Marbles', *Reuters News*, 23 May 2000.

[7] 'Zemin favours return of Parthenon marbles', *Agence France-Presse*, 22 April 2000.

[8] Trevor Marshallsea, 'Australian committee campaign for Greece's lost marbles', *Australian Associated Press*, 2 February 2000.

[9] Britain agreed to sign this in 2015, but at the time of writing has yet to do so.

[10] David Hencke, 'Greek snub to British Museum over marbles', *The Guardian*, 5 December 2000.

the British Museum's actions as a crass misuse of one of the world's greatest antiquities.[11]

The Parthenon Sculptures were made for a place of worship. The head of the British Museum's public relations department, which promoted the dinners, was amazed there should be such reactions against the dinners and defended the museum's practice. He was quoted as saying, 'We only allow the Duveen Gallery for dinners for very serious fundraisers and responsible wealthy individuals at £35,000 a time … As for themed dinners these can be very tasteful and the clothes must be responsible – there is no nudity or revealing clothes.'[12]

---

[11] David Hencke, 'Museum slated over parties with the Marbles' *The Guardian* 8 November 1999, p. 1.

[12] Hencke, 'Museum slated over parties with the Marbles', *The Guardian* 8 November 1999, p. 1.

CHAPTER 26

Further reading

The British Museum's pamphlet 'The Parthenon Sculptures' provides key information for understanding the history of the Parthenon, and includes short sections covering, 'What has the Greek government asked for?' and 'What is the British Museum's position?'[1] Readers interested in finding out more about the Parthenon debate are referred to the British Museum's website and to the website of the Hellenic Ministry of Culture.[2]

The British Museum's pamphlet recommends seven books as 'Further reading'. There is no balance in the books recommended. Five of the seven books are written by employees of the British Museum, and all five are published by the British Museum Press. The addition of, say, *The Parthenon Marbles: The Case for Reunification* by Christopher Hitchens would add a modicum of balance to the reading list.[3]

---

[1] 'The Parthenon Sculptures.' *The British Museum.* <www.britishmuseum.org/about_us/news_and_press/statements/parthenon_sculptures.aspx>. Last accessed: 27 July 2016.

[2] *The British Museum* (www.britishmuseum.co.uk) and *Hellenic Ministry of Culture and Sport* (www.culture.gr).

[3] Christopher Hitchens, *The Parthenon Marbles: The Case for Reunification* (London: Verso, 2008).

CHAPTER 27

Transplanting ancient Greece into England

In 1634, Henry Peacham (poet and writer) claimed that antiquities were difficult to obtain in Italy because of strict laws preventing their exportation, 'but in Greece ... they may be had for digging and carrying'.[1] This is what was happening. Peacham wrote of an English nobleman who took antiquities from Greece and continued to 'transplant old Greece into England'.[2]

Two hundred years after Peacham, Adolf Michaelis, a German classical scholar, catalogued the Greek and Roman antiquities transported to Britain. He visited the British Museum and ninety-three private collections, after which he confidently claimed, 'Peacham's saying about transplanting of old Greece into England had been realized'.[3]

No corner of ancient Greece and none of Greece's antiquities were spared in transplanting old Greece into England. The British government and the trustees of the British Museum were largely responsible for taking Greek antiquities. Consider, as an example, the British Museum collection of ancient Greek inscriptions. Inscriptions were sawed from marble and stone temples and edifices using stone saws and mason's grit. The British Museum sent saws to individuals who acted under the directions of the trustees of the British Museum and who were funded by the British government. The following

---

[1] Henry Peacham, *The Compleat Gentleman.* Reprint of 1634 edn (Oxford: Clarendon Press, 1906), p. 107.

[2] Peacham, *The Compleat Gentleman*, p. 107.

[3] Adolf Michaelis, *Ancient Marbles in Great Britain.* Trans. from the German by Charles Fennell (Cambridge: Cambridge University Press, 1882), p. xiii.

are two examples of saws sent by the British Museum specifically to be used to cut inscriptions.

The first, sixty tons of sculptured marble, was taken from the classical Greek site of the Temple of Diana at Ephesus in Turkey by John Turtle Wood. He was employed there for eleven years by the trustees of the British Museum and funded by the government.[4] In a letter to *The Times*, Wood wrote that he conducted 'the excavations at Ephesus for the Trustees of the British Museum'.[5] In his account of his excavations he explained, under a section headed 'Sawing Marble', that Antonio Panizzi, the Principal Librarian and Secretary of the British Museum, sent him stone-cutting saws, and when he received the saws:

> I at once proceeded to make the best use I could, by sawing off slabs from bulky stones ... I thus secured all that was worth sending, and considerably reduced the cost of their transport to England both in the number and sizes of the cases, and the amount of freight.[6]

Wood names four H. M. Ships that transported 'between 50 and 60 tons of sculptured stones and inscriptions' to the British Museum. He sent the British Museum more than four hundred inscriptions. The Temple of Diana was one of the Seven Wonders of the Ancient World. It was destroyed in 356 BC, rebuilt more than once and, finally, mutilated by Wood under the direction of the trustees of the British Museum.

The second example of saws being sent by the British Museum also involves Panizzi. He requested that the Admiralty deliver equipment, which included two stone saws and mason's grit for use with the saws, to Lieutenant Robert Murdoch Smith and Lieutenant Edwin A. Porcher.[7] The two were looking for antiquities for the British Museum in Cyrenaica (North Africa), colonised by the Greeks and Romans. Their explorations in

---

4 'British Museum', in Treasury: Registers of Papers, 1868, NA, T2/282.

5 J. T. Wood, 'Letter to the Editor: Our Consul at Smyrna', *The Times*, 8 July 1872, p. 12.

6 J. T. Wood, *Discoveries at Ephesus, Including the Site and Remains of the Great Temple of Diana* (London: Longmans, Green, and Co., 1877), p. 206.

7 Miscellaneous Letters (incl. British Museum), 1861, NA, ADM 1/5777.

Cyrenaica were funded by the British government and 'carried on under the direction of the trustees of the British Museum'.[8] Smith and Porcher wrote an account of their excavations in which they list over sixty inscriptions.[9]

Another source of Greek inscriptions for the British Museum was Charles Thomas Newton. He was employed at the British Museum for twelve years before being appointed acting British Consul at Rhodes in 1852 and then Vice Consul at Mytilene (on the Greek island of Lesbos), controlled by Turkey at the time. Newton published an account of his discoveries in which he wrote, 'In receiving this appointment from the Foreign Office, I was, at the same time *instructed* to use such opportunities as presented themselves for the acquisition of Antiquities for the British Museum' [emphasis added].[10] He continued:

> During my official residence in Turkey from 1852 to 1859 as Vice Consul of Mytilene I was able to obtain one hundred and fifty-eight inscriptions from the islands of Mytilene, Kalymna, Kos, Rhodes, Kasos and from the sites of Halicarnassus, Cnidus, and Branchidae on the west coast of Asia Minor.[11]

Newton returned to the British Museum, where he remained for twenty-seven years as Keeper of the Greek and Roman Antiquities.

Newton, Smith and Porcher, Wood and others, acting under the direction of the trustees of the British Museum and funded by the government, took more, of course, than Greek inscriptions, but inscriptions are used here as an example to illustrate the extent to which ancient Greece was transplanted to England.

---

[8] Newton, ed. *The Collection of Ancient Greek Inscriptions in the British Museum*, Part I, Preface, n.p.

[9] Robert Murdoch Smith and Edwin Augustus Porcher, *History of the Recent Discoveries at Cyrene Made during an Expedition to the Cyrenaica in 1860–61, under the Auspices of Her Majesty's Government* (London: Day & Son, 1864), Appendix IV, 'Inscriptions discovered or found at Cyrene with translations', p. 148 onwards.

[10] C. T. Newton, *Travels and Discoveries in the Levant* (London: Day & Son, 1865), Preface, n.p.

[11] Newton, ed. *The Collection of Ancient Greek Inscriptions in the British Museum*, Preface, n.p.

In 1874, the British Museum catalogued, in four volumes, its Greek inscriptions that had been taken from: Athens (from the Parthenon and other temples), Argolis, Arkadia, Boeotia, Bosphoros, Corcyra, Crete, Cyprus, Delos, Ios, Kalymna, Karpathos, Kasos, Kimmeria, Kos, Kythira, Laconia, Lesbos, Macedonia, Megara, Melos, Mytilene, Rhodes, Samos, Siphnos, Telos, Tenos, Thasos, Thessaly, Thrace; and from Greek sites in Turkey: Branchidae, Ephesus, Halicarnassus, Iasos, Kindos and Priene.[12]

Greek inscriptions and sculptures go hand in hand. The British Museum has sculptures from every single one of the above named places.

Newton, as Keeper of Greek and Roman Antiquities, explained how the collection was formed: 'It has been acquired by purchase, by donations, and also through the exploration of ancient sites, conducted by the Government, by the Trustees, or by private enterprise.'[13] The role of the government and trustees of the British Museum has, in part, been covered above. With regard to private enterprise, Elgin's Collection of Marbles acquired by the British Museum in 1816 included 'upwards of a hundred highly interesting inscriptions, mostly from Athens'.[14]

Thousands of inscriptions were sawed from sublime temples and edifices under the direction of the trustees of the British Museum, leaving innumerable mutilated temples and other buildings. There was a catastrophic loss of cultural heritage and property – and to what end? The thousands of Greek inscriptions in the British Museum have, with few exceptions, been in storage since the day they arrived in London. For example, in 2012 only three of the over four hundred inscriptions taken from Ephesus were on display, and even then they were placed in a small basement (Room 78, Classical Inscriptions) with few visitors. As with much else at the British Museum, the inscriptions have been hoarded and stored out of their cultural context. Inscriptions lose much of their meaning

---

[12] Newton, ed. *The Collection of Ancient Greek Inscriptions in the British Museum*, Parts I, II, III & IV.

[13] Newton, ed. *The Collection of Ancient Greek Inscriptions in the British Museum*, Preface, n.p.

[14] Newton, ed. *The Collection of Ancient Greek Inscriptions in the British Museum*, Preface, n.p.

when they are hacked from the temples on which they were intended to be read with the surrounding mountains, sea and sky.

The sculptured marbles on the Parthenon formed part of the supreme monument of Greek antiquity. The concerted effort to take them to England was not a one-off isolated incident. It was part of the obsession, first noted in 1634, to transplant old Greece into England. There is absolutely no way the Parthenon Sculptures would be left behind.

Newton wrote candidly of the active role played by the government and trustees of the British Museum in taking Greek antiquities. Primary sources establish that both were actively involved. The taking of the Parthenon Sculptures should be viewed in a new light.

CHAPTER 28

UNESCO and the Elgin Marbles

The Parthenon is a UNESCO World Heritage Site. UNESCO, the United Nations Educational, Scientific and Cultural Organization, is known as the 'intellectual' agency of the United Nations. UNESCO's activities cover education, natural and human sciences, culture, communication, freedom of the press, cultural diversity and natural heritage.

In August 2013, UNESCO wrote to Britain's Foreign Secretary, the Secretary of State for Culture, Media and Sport, and the Director of the British Museum urging all three to take part in a mediation procedure with Greece, facilitated by UNESCO, in a diplomatic bid to resolve the long-running dispute over the Parthenon Sculptures.

On 26 March 2015, nineteen months after UNESCO's offer to mediate, the British Museum replied in an open letter. It told UNESCO, in the nicest possible way, to mind its own business. The British Museum pointed out that UNESCO's role, as an intergovernmental agency, was to address the issue of threats to, and the destruction of, cultural heritage around the world. Clearly the Parthenon Sculptures preserved in the British Museum, and in other museums in Europe, did not fall into this category. The British Museum respectfully declined UNESCO's offer to mediate.[1]

---

[1] Sir Richard Lambert, Chairman of the British Museum Board of Trustees, to Alfredo Pérez de Armiñán, Assistant Director-General for Culture, UNESCO, 26 March 2015. 'The Parthenon Sculptures in the British Museum: UNESCO mediation proposal', *The British Museum*. <www.britishmuseum.org/about_us/news_and_press/press_releases/2015/unesco_mediation_proposal.aspx>. Last accessed: 30 July 2016.

However, UNESCO has assisted in the return of objects that were clearly being carefully preserved and were not under any risk.[2] For example, in 1983 UNESCO assisted in the return by Italy of over 12,000 pre-Columbian objects to Ecuador. These objects were being carefully preserved in Italy. As another example, in 1987 UNESCO assisted in the return of 7,000 Bogazköy cuneiform tablets from Germany to Turkey. These tablets, too, were being carefully preserved in Germany. UNESCO also assisted in the return of 271 objects from the United States to the Museum of Corinth in Greece. Once again the objects were carefully preserved. UNESCO is not precluded from offering assistance to mediate in restitution cases merely because the objects in question are carefully preserved.

The British Museum's letter to UNESCO further suggested that the 'historic distribution' of the Parthenon Sculptures in European museums was a very good thing because it meant that more people got to see them. There is no doubt that the dispersal throughout the world of the British Museum collections, consisting of about eight million objects, the overwhelming majority of which are in perpetual storage, would be a good thing for the same reason. Of course, this would not wash with the British Museum, which is happy to apply the argument in respect of the Parthenon Sculptures. In any event, the British Museum's argument, that the historic distribution of the sculptures is a good thing, is absurd. This is because the Parthenon Frieze is a continuous band of sculpture with a narrative, the Great Panathenaic Procession, intended to be viewed as a whole. The British Museum's contention is akin to suggesting that China's terracotta soldiers should be dispersed to thousands of museums worldwide so that everyone can have the opportunity of seeing one of them.

On the same day as the British Museum rejected UNESCO's offer, the Foreign & Commonwealth Office (Department for Culture, Media and Sport) also responded to the UNESCO offer to mediate made nineteen months earlier. The open letter points out that the trustees of the British Museum are prevented

---

[2] This has been done under UNESCO's Intergovernmental Committee for Promoting the Return of Cultural Property to its Countries of Origin or its Restitution in case of Illicit Appropriation.

by law from disposing of objects in the collection. This is once again placing reliance on the artificial barrier created by the British Museum Act 1963, a barrier created with the Elgin Marbles in mind.

The Foreign & Commonwealth Office said it was keen to cooperate with UNESCO, but it was a fact that the Parthenon Sculptures in the British Museum were legally acquired by Elgin under the laws pertaining at the time and that the British Museum has clear legal title. The letter added that neither the British government nor the British Museum were aware of any new arguments to dispute this since 1985, when the government last considered and rejected a request to return the marbles to Greece.[3]

However, the facts stated by the Foreign & Commonwealth Office – that the marbles were legally acquired by Elgin under the laws pertaining at the time and that the British Museum has clear legal title – are wrong.

In the Elgin Marbles Debate of 1816, it was forcefully expressed in the House of Commons that there had been spoliation and robbery and that Elgin had not acquired the marbles legally. The amount paid by Elgin as 'Commission and Agency ... in Turkey' was deleted from his expenses published as Appendix 5 of the Select Committee Report. Why would this line be deleted if there was nothing to hide? The said omission and deletion is clear evidence that it was known that Elgin did not acquire the marbles legally.

If the marbles were not legally acquired, then Elgin did not have title to the marbles, and they were not Elgin's to sell to the British Museum. This was acknowledged by the British government when it agreed to pay Elgin only the expenses incurred in obtaining the marbles, and then immediately recouped those expenses (via the mortgage over the marbles) since it, not Elgin, had paid for all of the expenses, including bribes to obtain the marbles.

---

[3] Ed Vaizey MP and Rt Hon David Lidington MP to Alfredo Pérez de Armiñán, Assistant Director-General for Culture UNESCO, 26 March 2015. 'The Parthenon Sculptures in the British Museum: UNESCO mediation proposal', *The British Museum*.
<https://www.britishmuseum.org/pdf/150326_Parthenon_Sculptures_in_the_British_Museum_DCMS_and_FCO.pdf>. Last accessed: 30 July 2016.

It is impossible for the British Museum to have clear legal title to the marbles as claimed by the Foreign & Commonwealth Office because Elgin never had title to give. It is a common law principle, *nemo dat quod non habet* – 'no one can give what he does not have'. Elgin clearly did not have legal title to the marbles taken from the Parthenon. If he had title he could have sold them close to Canova's valuation of £100,000. If Elgin's title was defective then so too is the British Museum's.

In 2005, the High Court (Chancery Division) considered the statutory prohibition on the British Museum disposing of objects in the collections. The case, *Attorney General v Trustees of the British Museum (Commission for Looted Art in Europe intervening)*, concerned four Old Master Drawings acquired by the British Museum at auction that were subsequently established to have been looted by the Gestapo.[4]

The trustees of the British Museum considered it morally right that the drawings should be returned to the owner's heirs, but the British Museum Act 1963 prevented them from doing so. At the time, the Holocaust (Return of Cultural Objects) Act 2009 was not yet law. So the issue before the High Court was whether the Attorney General or the court had power to authorise the return of the drawings to the rightful owner. The restriction in Section 3(4) of the British Museum Act 1963 applies to 'Objects vested in the trustees *as part of the collections of the museum* [emphasis added]'. In the High Court, Sir Andrew Morritt V-C held that neither the Crown nor the Attorney General, as a minister of the Crown, had power to dispense with the due observance of Acts of Parliament. Therefore, the drawings could not be returned by the British Museum. However, one of Sir Andrew Morritt's conclusions was that if the heirs of the owner of the drawings could establish title to the drawings with the consequence that the drawings would never have been 'part of the collections of the museum', then Section 3(4) of the British Museum Act 1963 would not preclude the trustees from returning the drawings.[5] This means that if Elgin never had title to the Elgin Marbles, then neither does the

---

[4] *Attorney General v Trustees of the British Museum (Commission for Looted Art in Europe intervening)* [2005] EWHC 1089 (Ch), *Weekly Law Reports* (2005), vol. 3, p. 396.

[5] *Attorney General v Trustees of the British Museum*, paragraph 38.

British Museum; therefore, the marbles cannot be 'part of the collections of the museum'. This means the Parthenon Sculptures can be returned to Greece without needing to remove the artificial barrier in the British Museum Act 1963.

If the case to retain the Elgin Marbles is as clear-cut and as watertight as is made out by the Foreign & Commonwealth Office and the British Museum in their replies to UNESCO, then why not take part in UNESCO's mediation? UNESCO's mediation is non-binding. What is there to fear?

In May 2016, the Greek government hoped that the United Nations would assist in recovering the Parthenon Sculptures.[6] The world's most important unresolved cultural property issue is not going away.

---

[6] Helena Smith, 'Greece looks to UN in Parthenon marbles row', *The Guardian*, 9 May 2016, p. 7.

CHAPTER 29

'Was the acquisition legal?'

In 2014, *The Times* published an article under the headline, 'The Marbles are not Greek. They don't need reuniting. The acquisition was legal. We do the same deals today.'[1] The four statements were made by Neil MacGregor, at the time the Director of the British Museum. In the article, MacGregor explained why the Elgin Marbles could not be returned to Greece.

To begin to grasp the argument that the Elgin Marbles are not Greek, consider Stonehenge not being Britain's, or England's, on the grounds that neither Britain nor England existed when Stonehenge was built. When construction of the Parthenon began in 447 BC London did not exist, other than as a settlement on the marshy banks of the Thames. Yet the Parthenon Sculptures in the British Museum are bizarrely claimed by some to be part of Britain's heritage for no other reason than that they have been under the British Museum's roof. The Crown Jewels can *never* become part of another country's national heritage by being held in another country, no matter for how long.

The British Museum definitively does not do the same deals as the Elgin Marbles deal today, despite what MacGregor claimed in the 2014 article. To suggest that the museum does betrays a lack of understanding of what took place.

Was the Elgin Marbles deal legal as is claimed? In Tiffany Jenkins's book *Keeping their Marbles: How the treasures of the past ended up in museums...and why they should stay there,* it is

---

[1] Richard Morrison, 'The Marbles are not Greek. They don't need reuniting. The acquisition was legal. We do the same deals today', *The Times 2 Arts,* 7 November 2014, pp. 4–5.

maintained on the second page that few doubt the legal right of the British Museum to retain the Elgin Marbles.[2] The above article pointed out that MacGregor was a Scottish-trained solicitor and that he posed a question which he answered. MacGregor asked if the acquisition was legal; he answered that he thought everybody would have to agree it was legal. Not everybody – in Elgin's day hardly anyone agreed it was legal. And now?

Elgin took sculptures from the Parthenon with financial assistance from the government, which included transportation by the Admiralty. After this, the government resorted to openly funding the British Museum to enable individuals to take Greek antiquities for the museum. This is beyond any doubt, because Treasury funding for Newton, Wood, Smith and Porcher at the sites they excavated is recorded in British Museum Annual Accounts presented to parliament. However, when the Elgin Marbles were taken, the government acted covertly and the government slipped up. This is because the government failed to ensure that the British Museum got title to the Elgin Marbles.

In order to safeguard the Elgin Marbles in the British Museum, an intermediary buyer should have been inserted between Elgin and the British Museum. The Elgin Marbles should have been warehoused with a third party for years to disassociate the British Museum from Elgin.

However, in 1816 there was an urgency to get the Elgin Marbles into the British Museum. As Mr Rose stated in the House of Commons the previous year, the trustees of the British Museum 'were determined' to get the Elgin Marbles.[3] Because of the urgency, the legislative process, from the Marbles Debate to the Act of Parliament receiving the Royal Assent, took just twenty-four days and the trustees immediately had the marbles.

The British Museum's claim that the marble sculptures were purchased by the British parliament from Elgin and presented by parliament to the British Museum distances the British

---

[2] Tiffany Jenkins, *Keeping their Marbles: How the treasures of the past ended up in museums…and why they should stay there* (Oxford: Oxford University Press, 2016), p. 2.

[3] Petition of the Earl of Elgin respecting his Collection of Marbles, HC Deb, 15 June 1815, vol. 31, col. 830.

Museum from Elgin.[4] The claim is incorrect, but it does enable, for example, John Henry Merryman, Emeritus and Affiliated Professor in the Department of Art at Stanford Law School, to maintain that the British government bought the marbles from Elgin. Furthermore, it enables Merryman to discuss the right of the Crown to the Elgin Marbles and the Crown's title to the marbles.[5]

Merryman makes a strong case for the British Museum retaining the Elgin Marbles, but qualifies it with, 'unless a quite different version of the facts were found'.[6] He states that he relied on the following:

- 'The British government bought the Marbles from Lord Elgin in 1816 after a full discussion in Parliament, in full knowledge of the facts.' In a footnote Merryman says that 'the facts are fully set out' in the Select Committee Report.[7]
- 'If Lord Elgin owned the Marbles, he could transfer ownership to the Crown. If his title was defective, then so was the Crown's title.'[8]
- 'The Select Committee inquired whether Elgin got the Marbles as British Minister or in his personal capacity and decided the latter: hence the purchase by Parliament.'[9]

Merryman adds a footnote: 'It is possible that the facts are different.'[10] The facts are indeed different. Parliament did *not* buy the marbles from Elgin (the Crown never had title to the Marbles). The Select Committee did *not* decide that Elgin got the marbles in a personal capacity. Parliament did *not* have full knowledge of the facts. Parliament was completely misled as to the government's role in obtaining the marbles.

---

[4] 'What are the "Elgin Marbles"?' *The British Museum.* Last accessed: 17 October 2014. No longer available.

[5] Merryman, *Thinking about the Elgin Marbles,* p. 36.

[6] Merryman, *Thinking about the Elgin Marbles,* p. 42.

[7] Merryman, *Thinking about the Elgin Marbles,* p. 36 and n. 46.

[8] Merryman, *Thinking about the Elgin Marbles,* p. 36.

[9] Merryman, *Thinking about the Elgin Marbles,* p. 42.

[10] Merryman, *Thinking about the Elgin Marbles,* p. 42 n. 78.

The Member of Parliament Mr Hammersley was right two hundred years ago when he said during the Elgin Marbles Debate, 'We should not place in our museum a monument of our disgrace.'[11]

[11] Elgin Marbles, HC Deb, 7 June 1816, vol. 34, col. 1027.

Bibliography

Primary sources

An Act to vest the Elgin Collection of ancient Marbles and Sculpture in the Trustees of the British Museum for the Use of the Public (1816). Public Act, 56 George III, c. 99. <discovery.nationalarchives.gov.uk/details/rd/647d80ec-79a1-4cca-8383-2302cbf08c63>.

Historic Hansard (1803–2005). <hansard.millbanksystems.com/commons/>. (House of Commons and House of Lords debates.)

National Archives, Public Record Office, Kew, London (NA): Admiralty papers; Chancery papers; Foreign Office papers; Treasury papers.

Parliamentary Archives. Houses of Parliament, London. <www.parliament.uk/business/publications/parliamentary-archives/>

ProQuest U.K. Parliamentary Papers. <parlipapers.proquest.com/parlipapers>. (Institution/library subscription required).

Secondary sources

Attorney General v Trustees of the British Museum (Commission for Looted Art in Europe intervening) [2005] EWHC 1089 (Ch), *Weekly Law Reports* (2005), vol. 3, p. 396.

Beard, Mary. *The Parthenon.* Cambridge, MA.: Harvard University Press, 2002.

Cahill, Julia. 'British Museum in legal fight over Elgin Marbles', *The Lawyer,* 11 February 2002. < www.thelawyer.com/issues/11-february-2002/british-museum-in-legal-fight-over-elgin-marbles/>. Accessed: 25 July 2016.

'Captain Perry, of the *Lady Shaw Stewart*', *The Times*, 20 May 1806, p. 3.

Catalogue of the Antiquities in the Earl of Elgin's Museum. London: Reynell printed for private circulation, 1815.

Checkland, Sydney G. *The Elgins, 1766–1917: A Tale of Aristocrats, Proconsuls and their Wives.* Aberdeen: Aberdeen University Press, 1988.

Clarke, Edward D. *Travels in Various Countries of Europe, Asia and Africa. Part 2 Greece, Egypt and the Holy Land.* London: T. Cadell and W. Davies, 1814.

Coates, Sam. 'Public split by museum's decision to lend Marbles', *The Times*, 9 December 2014, p. 7.

'Conservation Case Studies: Cleaning Theseus and the Minotaur.' 25 July 2013. *Victoria and Albert Museum.* <www.vam.ac.uk/content/articles/c/cleaning-theseus-and-the-minotaur/>. Accessed: 26 July 2016.

Cook, B. F. *The Elgin Marbles.* London: British Museum Press, 1997.

Davenport, Hugo. 'Elgin Marbles surprise', *The Observer*, 15 May 1983, p. 4.

Diana Douse and John Woodhouse. 'The Parthenon Sculptures.' *www.parliament.uk.* 13 December 2012. <researchbriefings.files.parliament.uk/documents/SN02075/SN02075.pdf>. Accessed: 25 July 2916.

Elgin, Lord. 'The Present Lord Elgin Tots Up the Bill for Those Marbles' [Letter to the Editor], *New York Times*, 7 November 1971, p. 4.

Gallo, Luciana. *Lord Elgin and Ancient Greek Architecture: The Elgin Drawings at the British Museum.* Cambridge: Cambridge University Press, 2009.

'Heidelberg frieze fragment return & its implications for the Elgin Marbles.' *Elginism.* 12 September 2006. <www.elginism.com/elgin-marbles/heidelberg-frieze-fragment-implications-for-the-elgin-marbles/20060912/535/>. Accessed: 26 July 2016.

Hellenic Ministry of Culture and Sports. <www.culture.gr>.

Hencke, David. 'Greek snub to British Museum over marbles', *The Guardian,* 5 December 2000.

_____. 'Museum slated over parties with the Marbles', *The Guardian* 8 November 1999, p. 1.

Hirst, Sir David. 'Report of the Spoliation Advisory Panel in respect of four drawings now in the possession of the British Museum.' 27 April 2006. *The British Museum.* <www.britishmuseum.org/pdf/spoliationreport_fourdrawings_2006.pdf>. Accessed: 30 July 2016.

Hitchens, Christopher. *The Parthenon Marbles: The Case for Reunification.* London: Verso, 2008.

Hoyle, Ben, and Jack Malvern. 'Elgin Marbles moved out of Britain for first time', *The Times,* 5 December 2014, p. 1.

Jenkins, Tiffany. *Keeping their Marbles: how the treasures of the past ended up in museums…and why they should stay there.* Oxford: Oxford University Press, 2016.

[Lord Keith at Malta]. *The Times,* 20 February 1802, p. 2.

[Lord Keith at St. Helen's]. *The Times,* 6 July 1802, p. 2.

Malvern, Jack, and Ben Hoyle. 'Greece slams UK for loan of statue', *The Times,* 6 December 2014, p. 1.

Marshallsea, Trevor. 'Australian committee campaign for Greece's lost marbles', *Australian Associated Press,* 2 February 2000.

Memorandum on the Subject of the Earl of Elgin's Pursuits in Greece. Edinburgh: Balfour, Kirkwood, & Co., 1810.

Merryman, John Henry. *Thinking about the Elgin Marbles: Critical Essays on Cultural Property, Art and Law.* 2nd ed. The Hague: Kluwer Law International, 2009.

Michaelis, Adolf. *Ancient Marbles in Great Britain.* Trans. from the German by Charles Fennell. Cambridge: Cambridge University Press, 1882.

_____. *Der Parthenon.* Leipzig: Breitkopf und Härtel, 1870–71.

Morrison, Richard. 'The Marbles are not Greek. They don't need reuniting. The acquisition was legal. We do the same deals today', *The Times 2 Arts*, 7 November 2014, pp. 4–5.

Morritt, John B. S. *The Letters of John B.S. Morritt of Rokeby: Descriptive of Journeys in Europe and Asia Minor in the Years 1794–1796.* London: John Murray, 1914.

Newton, C. T. ed. *The Collection of Ancient Greek Inscriptions in the British Museum.* Oxford: The Clarendon Press, 1874.

Newton, C. T. *Travels and Discoveries in the Levant.* London: Day & Son, 1865.

'No Losing the marbles: The Parthenon sculptures should remain at the British Museum', [Opinion piece], *The Times*, 14 October 2014, p. 30.

Oxford Dictionary of National Biography. <www.oxforddnb.com/>.

Oxford Journal, 5 March 1803.

Peacham, Henry. *The Compleat Gentleman.* Reprint of 1634 edn. Oxford: Clarendon Press, 1906.

'Plymouth', *Exeter Flying Post* ,19 August 1802, p. 4.

Report from the Select Committee of the House of Commons on the Earl of Elgin's Collection of Sculptured Marbles; &c. (London: W. Bulmer, 1816).

St Clair, William. *Lord Elgin and the Marbles*, 1st edn. Oxford: Oxford University Press, 1967.

Seltman, Charles. 'Two Athenian Marble Thrones', *Journal of Hellenic Studies*, 67 (November 1947), pp. 22–30.

'Ship News Plymouth', *Hampshire Chronicle*, 9 March 1801, p. 4.

'Ship News', *Morning Chronicle*, 11 July 1812, p. 3.

'Should the Parthenon Sculptures be returned?' *Museums Association.* < www.museumsassociation.org/museums-journal/news/01062012-should-parthenon-marbles-be-returned-to-greece>. Last accessed: 27 July 2016.

Smith, A. H. 'Lord Elgin and his Collection', *Journal of Hellenic Studies*, 36 (November 1916), pp. 163–372.

Smith, Helena. 'Greece looks to UN in Parthenon marbles row', *The Guardian*, 9 May 2016, p. 7.

Smith, Capt. R. Murdoch, and Commander E. A. Porcher. *History of the Recent Discoveries at Cyrene Made during an Expedition to the Cyrenaica in 1860–61, under the Auspices of Her Majesty's Government.* London: Day & Son, 1864.

'Speech of the Minister of Culture Mr Georgios Voulgarakis at the Presentation of the First Fragment of the Parthenon Marbles that was returned in Greece by the University of Heidelberg.' *Hellenic Ministry of Culture and Sports.* 5 September 2006. <odysseus.culture.gr/a/1/12/files/omilia_05_09_06_en.pdf>. Accessed: 26 July 2016.

Steel, David. *Steel's Original and Correct List of the Royal Navy.* London: Steel's Navigation Warehouse, 1812.

'Sunday's Post', *Hampshire Chronicle*, 23 April 1804, p. 4.

The British Museum. <www.britishmuseum.org>.

'The Parthenon Sculptures in the British Museum: UNESCO mediation proposal.' *The British Museum.* <www.britishmuseum.org/about_us/news_and_press/press_releases/2015/unesco_mediation_proposal.aspx>. Accessed: 30 July 2016.

'The Parthenon Sculptures: Facts and Figures.' *The British Museum.* 2008. <www.britishmuseum.org/about_us/news_and_press/statements/parthenon_sculptures/facts_and_figures.aspx>. Accessed 25 July 2016.

'The Parthenon Sculptures.' *The British Museum.* <www.britishmuseum.org/about_us/news_and_press/statements/parthenon_sculptures.aspx>. Accessed: 27 July 2016.

'The restitution of the Parthenon Marbles: The review of the seizure.' *Hellenic Ministry of Culture and Sports.* <odysseus.culture.gr/a/1/12/ea125.html>. Accessed: 26 July 2016.

The Royal Kalendar. London: J. Debrett, 1800.

The Royal Kalendar. London: J. Debrett, 1815.

'Turkey backs Greek fight to regain Elgin Marbles', *Reuters News,* 5 February 2000.

'US First Lady asks Britain to return Elgin Marbles', *Reuters News,* 23 May 2000.

'What are the "Elgin Marbles"?' *The British Museum.* Last accessed: 17 October 2014. No longer available.

Wilson, David M. *The British Museum – A History.* London: The British Museum Press, 2002.

Wood, J. T. 'Letter to the Editor: Our Consul at Smyrna', *The Times,* 8 July 1872, p. 12.

_____. *Discoveries at Ephesus, Including the Site and Remains of the Great Temple of Diana.* London: Longmans, Green, and Co., 1877.

'Zemin favours return of Parthenon marbles', *Agence France-Presse,* 22 April 2000.

INDEX